Emotions: Mirrors of the heart

The heart matters. It's the fountain of our personality from which everything flows. The deeply-embedded attitudes of our hearts are the key to wisdom, godly character and healthy living – or otherwise. Illustrated from her own experience and a number of case studies, Catherine offers us a sure-footed guide through the minefield of our own fallen and fickle feelings. Her sanctified version of CBT offers us a way of both understanding and managing them. We don't need to fear our emotions; they are God-given indicators to what's going on in our hearts. Best of all, he is at work in them and through them to make us more like Jesus. A good read for everyone involved in helping others to walk with him. That should be all of us, then!

– Richard Underwood, Pastoral Ministries Director, FIEC

It sometimes feels like the 'noise' of our emotions can drown out any rational thought about why we are reacting as we do. Emotions, Mirrors of the Heart gives a handy model to help us to get to the heart of why we feel the way we do and apply the Bible's truth there. I can see myself keeping these ideas in my back pocket for conversations with strugglers, including myself.

– Agnes Brough, Associate Minister for Women and Young People, The Tron Church, Glasgow

EMOTIONS

MIRRORS OF THE HEART

Hope for those in the grip of powerful emotions

Catherine Haddow

10 Publishing
a division of 10 of those.com

First published in Great Britain in 2017

British Library Cataloguing in Publication Data
A record for this book is available from the British Library

ISBN: 978-1-911272-84-7

Designed by Jude May at www.judemaydesign.com

Printed in the UK

10Publishing, a division of 10ofthose.com
Unit C, Tomlinson Road, Leyland, PR25 2DY, England
Email: info@10ofthose.com
Website: www.10ofthose.com

Contents

Acknowledgements

I would like to express my sincere thanks to the following people for their support and help in bringing this book into being:

To my wonderful husband, Richard, for his godly wisdom and leadership in our family *and* his patient proofreading and grammar checking.
To our lovely children, Sophie, James and Kezzy, for all the heightened emotions they bring me, causing me to constantly examine my heart!
To my pastor, Ben Midgley, for always encouraging me, for pushing me out of my comfort zone and for coming up with the name 'tbH' to summarise the model I outline.
To Phil Taylor, for his endless patience in designing yet another diagram!
To Daniel Caballero, for preaching the words 'mirrors of the heart' which began the work in my own heart that resulted in this book.
To CCEF and Biblical Counselling UK, for their literature, teaching and wisdom – as well as for opening my eyes to the privilege of serving the Lord through biblical counselling ministry.
To Julie Hatherall, for her biblical wisdom and editorial guidance.

Introduction

Above all else, guard your heart, for everything you do flows from it.

Proverbs 4:23

Picture this scene if you will. It's August and we are on a family holiday, spending a couple of weeks in the stunning Gower peninsular in south Wales. As our eldest daughter, Sophie, is on a Christian camp in the area for the first week, that leaves myself, my husband, Richard, James (aged ten) and Kezzy (aged six) to enjoy a week of family fun. For us this means heading to a beach. Armed with wet suits, bodyboards, equipment for building sandcastles and playing beach tennis plus books for me, it should be a perfect day out for us. We go to the beautiful Oxwich bay, the second largest beach on the peninsula, with almost three miles of golden sand stretching into the distance. What could be better? The problem is that on this particular day you can't even see the golden sand – or the sea for that matter. There is just a dull, grey band of low-lying, cold, wet cloud. Not only that but the weather forecast for the next ten days looks remarkably similar.

My husband, who is forever an optimist, has a favourite holiday expression that is, 'Look, there's a patch of blue sky over there …' He then drives us determinedly towards it. It's surprising how effective this approach usually is. However, today there are no patches of blue sky anywhere to head towards.

So instead Richard is adopting his second-favourite holiday phrase, which is, 'Let's find a stream to dam.' This is taken quite seriously in our family. However much the car looks to be standing up on its back wheels, weighed down by luggage for five, the metal garden spade will be added for damming.

Richard *thinks* he has read somewhere that on this beach there is a great river. So he is off on a mission to find it, determined that his family will still enjoy the holiday despite the weather. He's six feet three inches tall, thus resembling an overgrown version of one of the seven dwarfs as he strides off, a spade flung over his shoulder. He is a man on a mission and it isn't long before he is vanishing into the distance. I am following behind rather more slowly with the children, resembling a bag lady with a further collection of plastic spades and other beach necessities. After about two minutes there is the inevitable, 'Are we nearly there yet?' from Kezzy.

General moaning and complaining from the children continues for the next quarter of an hour, interspersed with my attempt at a cheery commentary to jolly them along. Of course, in my mind things aren't quite so cheery. Angry thoughts are rising, such as, 'What does he think he's doing? He doesn't even know for certain there is a river here.' I am rapidly losing my battle to motivate the children and myself forward. A feeling which had started as mild irritation is now mounting into one of fury.

To top it off, Kezzy encounters probably the biggest pile of dog mess on the beach. She then vanishes off into the sand dunes. James follows her. Kezzy subsequently reappears but there is no sight and (very unusually) no *sound* of James for some time. Kezzy has lost one of her shoes (permanently as it turns out). What's more, a large wasp has been my personal, very close companion for the last ten minutes.

At this point Richard enthusiastically bounces back, grinning away like an excited schoolboy. He's *found* the stream, he announces, and it is *great*. 'Just a bit further to go,' he declares, waving his hand vaguely into the distance. I glower at him, struggling to resist the overwhelming desire I have to whack him over the head with one of the five spades I am carrying. Kezzy moans, 'Aw, not further, Daddy.'

'What's wrong, Kez?' says Daddy brightly, his eyes glinting with pending dam anticipation. That's it. I see red.

'I'll tell you what's wrong with her,' I shout, and I launch into a detailed analysis of how I have been feeling for the last mile. Thankfully, due to the weather, the beach is totally deserted.

You may wonder why I am sharing this story with you. It's because as I'd been walking along with my mounting fury, I'd also had the opportunity – but had sadly failed – to start applying to myself some of the things I use in my professional work, namely to:

- Break down the unhelpful thoughts
- Acknowledge my sulky and stroppy demeanour towards my husband and children
- Acknowledge the fact that the same event was resulting in very different, positive thoughts and behaviour for my husband compared to mine
- Assess my heightened internal physiology
- Ultimately take a painful look at my heart and understand that my motivations and loyalty all pointed firmly at gratifying me
- Wonder at the purposes God had in placing me in this situation to change me

The idol of 'me' and 'my' perceived needs was gripping my heart, screaming at my hubby, 'I don't like this. This is hard for me and this is all *your* fault.' And, although I wasn't aware of it, I was also screaming at God, 'I am *not* going to rejoice in this situation you have intentionally placed me in'. I had failed to do what Proverbs 4:23 instructs us: 'Above all else, guard your heart, for everything you do flows from it.' My heart was all about *me* and what *I* wanted, and that certainly wasn't this awful walk along a beach on a miserable day. Everything about my thoughts, actions and emotions was flowing from my selfish heart desires and it wasn't a pretty sight.

This was a fairly brief glimpse into a heightened emotion flowing from the wellspring of my heart, and thankfully it was all over fairly quickly. But it is so easy to get caught up and enslaved by the difficult emotions we experience in daily life. This is especially true when they linger and occur regularly.

I work with people who are often crippled in their walk following Christ because of the overwhelming grip of their intense emotions. Perhaps some of you reading this book are aware that difficult emotions are a problem for you in your daily Christian walk? Or maybe you are involved in the pastoral care of others who are in the sway of difficult emotions?

My prayer is that from this book you will be equipped to understand more clearly your emotions, or those of others you support through pastoral care, as a mirror of the heart. But more than that, I pray that you will be guided to see how the beauty of God's love for us and his life-transforming grace shine through our brokenness and struggles as he gently moulds us into the likeness of his beloved Son, Jesus Christ.

1

Emotions as mirrors of the heart

The heart is deceitful above all things and beyond cure. Who can understand it?

Jeremiah 17:9

'Emotions are poor leaders, but good mirrors of the heart' – these were words preached in a sermon at my home church a few years ago and they made a profound impact on me. We live in a postmodern culture that is dominated by the pursuit of emotions, and their unique meaning for the individual experiencing them. But a biblical worldview of absolute truths turns postmodernism entirely on its head, as we will explore in this chapter.

We have deceptive hearts

The idea that emotions are poor at leading us but good at showing us our hearts cuts straight to the chase of the battle of the Christian life. Our emotions and heart can deceive us – they tell us what we want, which is not necessarily right or the truth, and encourage us to selfishly pursue our own agenda. Yet in motivating us in all that we do – for everything flows from our heart – they also highlight the essence of our sin. This shows us just how watchful we need to be of our emotions.

Jesus knows our hearts

Let's briefly look at how Jesus shows this to us. Mark 10:18–27 tells us the well-known story of the rich young man who asks Jesus how he can 'inherit eternal life' (v. 17). The young man has not grasped that eternal life is a gift from God rather than something he can inherit through works. He is confident in his salvation because he believes that he has kept God's commands perfectly from his youth. Jesus' reply that the young man should sell everything he owns and give it to the poor cuts straight to the heart of the problem and shows the rich man that he idolises money. The rich man, faced with the prospect of losing all that is dear to him, goes away 'sad' (v. 22). His heart idol – his love of money and all that it enables him to acquire – creates a powerful emotional attachment to all his worldly goods. When Jesus threatens his idol, he experiences extreme emotional discomfort. As Jesus comments to his disciples, 'Children, how hard it is to enter the kingdom of God! It is easier for a camel to go through the eye of a needle than for someone who is rich to enter the kingdom of God' (vv. 24–25).

The rich man's overt struggle to follow the second greatest command, 'Love your neighbour as yourself' (Mark 12:31), is revealed by his reluctance to give to the poor in the horizontal relational plane – that is to express his love to his fellow human beings. Moreover, this in turn clearly indicates his bigger covert struggle: to follow the most important command, 'Love the Lord your God with all your heart and with all your soul and with all your mind and with all your strength' (Mark 12:30). He is failing to love, on the vertical relational plane, the Lord his God. The question the rich man must face is who is he going to worship – God or his money?

What are our hearts saying?

We need to face up to similar questions about our own idols too.

Though our specific heart desires may be different from the rich young man, the emotions we feel and their associated outward behaviours are a language which communicate so much about the 'real us' and about what is truly going on in our hearts. Like the young man, we have the same choice to make about who we are going to worship. We need to decide if we are going to do things our way or God's way. The strong emotions we experience are in fact almost always a form of 'spiritual smoke alarm' going off. In the case of the difficult emotions this book considers, the alarm tells us that deep down, at a heart level, something needs addressing. Our daily interactions with others – on what could be termed the horizontal level – are a reflection of our vertical relationship with God. Our emotions are revealing something about our hearts, the 'real us', the 'us' that only God truly knows and what he most wants to change.

We are image bearers

However, I wouldn't want you to go away from reading this book thinking that emotions are bad. These are God-given, and to experience a full array of emotions is to be human and made in the image of God. The stoical attitude of an unemotional 'stiff upper lip' is not supported by Scripture. The Bible is full of individuals experiencing a vibrant array of emotions, both good and bad. The psalms reveal the phenomenal impact and depth of love, joy, contentment, pain, betrayal, compassion, grief, indignation, sorrow, fear, peace and thankfulness. Even experiencing some of the very difficult emotions listed here is not necessarily 'wrong'.

The key issue is that there is either a godly or a sinful way to manage our emotions. Emotions of all kinds can be good and biblical in energising us and driving us forward, but they can also lead us unhelpfully astray.

What exactly is an emotion?

It's perhaps useful at this point to clarify exactly what an emotion is. It's an elusive word that we hear a lot in everyday speech. When we get into discussions about emotions and feelings we can get tied in knots. Emotions are complicated as they are rarely felt in isolation. The boundaries between them are very blurred, for example someone displaying anger may actually also be very frightened. Also, our emotions are often something we find very hard to express verbally. So, to make sure we're all 'singing from the same hymn sheet', here's a couple of definitions for you:

A *dictionary* definition would describe emotions as a conscious mental reaction, subjectively experienced as a strong feeling, usually directed towards a specific object and typically accompanied by physiological and behavioural changes.

However, *the Bible* understands emotions as so much more than this. Our emotions reflect our image-bearing status of God, who experiences perfect emotions. Through the lens of Scripture, emotions are a language which force us – and others – to pay attention and respond. They provide invaluable communication about our inner selves and our true desires. And these desires are determined by the loyalties of our heart. Yet that language is sometimes very complicated for others and ourselves to decipher: our emotions are intertwined. They also communicate at two levels: on the horizontal about others, and on the vertical about God.

For the purpose of this book I will be using the terms 'emotion' and 'feeling' interchangeably.

Are our feelings reliable?

The answer to this is a resounding 'no': we cannot always trust our feelings. As a psychologist, I work with many people experiencing the grip of difficult emotions. I see first-hand the deep brokenness so many carry around as a result of being led and ruled by emotions. The weight and burden of suffering these feelings can so easily pull us away from our walk on the narrow road as we try to follow Jesus. For example, we see it in the:

- Teenage Christian girl who is sleeping with her boyfriend because they both prayed about it and they *felt* peaceful about it
- Young man who has left his third job in six months to head to Australia to be a pilot because he believes that God told him to do so and it *feels* right
- Young mum who hates herself because all she wants to do is shout at her children and doesn't *feel* they are a blessing from God
- Lady who can no longer read her Facebook page because she *feels* so worthless compared to everyone else's amazing lives
- Christians who are committing adultery because they *feel* God has fulfilled emotional needs through it that weren't met in their marriages
- Dear elderly man in his twilight years who doubts his salvation and where he will spend eternity because he *feels* low and has no joy

We can summarise the problem with following our feelings as follows:

> We are so easily led to believe that how we *feel* explains the reality of a situation. We believe that because we *feel* bad, the situation must *be* bad. Conversely, we *feel* good and therefore we conclude that the situation must *be* good. But the reality is that **because of the Fall, we think the wrong things, we do the wrong things, we desire the wrong things and we also feel the wrong things.**

A biblical worldview

As the summary above highlights, it is instead vital to look at our emotions through the framework of a biblical worldview – that is, through the lens of God's perfect creation, humankind's Fall and our redemption.

Creation

In Genesis 1 we see God creating a perfect world at the beginning of time and then two human beings to inhabit it. Genesis 1:27 says, 'So God created mankind in his own image, in the image of God he created them; male and female he created them.' Genesis 1:31 concludes, 'God saw all that he had made, and it was very good.' God created a perfect world and in Genesis 2 we view Adam and Eve living in perfect harmony with themselves, with each other and with God. How wonderful! We clearly see here a life free from doubts or fear and of perfect contentment with and acceptance of themselves and each other. It is also a life of direct communication and intimate relationship with God. Furthermore, in this world there is no death, no suffering (physical or emotional) or unhappiness, and no sin.

The Fall

Sadly, we know what happens next. God had given Adam and Eve the freedom to eat from all but one tree in the Garden of Eden (Genesis

2:16–17). Yet Eve took the forbidden fruit and ate it. Then she gave some to her husband and he ate it too. As Genesis 3:6–12 tells us:

When the woman saw that the fruit of the tree was good for food and pleasing to the eye, and also desirable for gaining wisdom, she took some and ate it. She also gave some to her husband, who was with her, and he ate it. Then the eyes of both of them were opened, and they realised they were naked; so they sewed fig leaves together and made coverings for themselves.
Then the man and his wife heard the sound of the LORD God as he was walking in the garden in the cool of the day, and they hid from the LORD God among the trees of the garden. But the LORD God called to the man, 'Where are you?'
He answered, 'I heard you in the garden, and I was afraid because I was naked; so I hid.'
And he said, 'Who told you that you were naked? Have you eaten from the tree from which I commanded you not to eat?'
The man said, 'The woman you put here with me – she gave me some fruit from the tree, and I ate it.'
Then the LORD God said to the woman, 'What is this you have done?'
The woman said, 'The snake deceived me, and I ate.'

Notice how following Eve's and then Adam's disobedience – the Fall – their perfect acceptance and belonging is immediately gone. Sin has entered the world, and the rest of Genesis 3 spells out that the consequence of this is death. Yet even now their life that had once been very good is replaced with physical and emotional suffering. The first indications of emotional discomfort are the shame Adam and Eve feel as their perceived weaknesses or defects in themselves are revealed publicly (v. 7). As a result their behaviour changes and they hide from God rather than talking with him (v. 8). Further discord arrives in the form of blame and guilt (vv. 11–13).

Of course, we too are fallen and therefore are sinful and fallible – in our thoughts, behaviour, desires *and* our emotions.

Redemption

However, although we are fallen, the wonderful news is that Jesus has come to save us, and free us from the guilt of sin. We have been rescued because Jesus, the perfect, sinless one, died on the cross and took the punishment for *our* sins – and not just our sins, but the sins of the whole world (1 John 2:2). Through his sacrificial death, we are free to live a new life through him and for him. The apostle Paul, addressing the church at Ephesus, puts it this way, 'In him we have redemption through his blood, the forgiveness of sins, in accordance with the riches of God's grace that he lavished on us' (Ephesians 1:7–8).

God, in his grace and mercy, has provided a way for us to be right with him again through Jesus. One day Jesus will return and take us to live forever with him and God the Father in the new heaven. As Revelation 21:3–4 tells us, when speaking of this future, 'God's dwelling-place is now among the people, and he will dwell with them. They will be his people, and God himself will be with them and be their God. "He will wipe every tear from their eyes. There will be no more death" or mourning or crying or pain, for the old order of things has passed away.' Furthermore, at this time we will be given new heavenly bodies and become like Jesus. This will include not only our character but also our emotions. We will be made pure and like Jesus in every way: in our thoughts, in our volition, in our deeds and in our emotions. 1 John 3:2–3 tells us, 'Dear friends, now we are children of God, and what we will be has not yet been made known. But we know that when Christ appears, we shall be like him, for we shall see him as he is. All who have this hope in him purify themselves, just as he is pure.'

The challenge for us now

Of course, this glorious future is not what we experience now. In the meantime, we must keep our eyes focused firmly on Christ whilst we experience the knocks and trials of life here on earth. Otherwise the trials can so often result in us being ruled and led by destructive feelings, such as the following:

- 'I can't *feel* God so he must have left me'
- 'How can I even call myself a Christian if I *feel* this way?'
- 'I thought Christians were supposed to *feel* joy – but I have none. What's wrong with me?'
- 'I must have done something really wrong for God to let me *feel* this way'

Whilst we are in this world, we will inevitably be hit with emotional turbulence from experiencing the trials of this life. Yet as our emotions are fallen, they cannot be trusted to lead us, though too often we let them do just that. It is so easy to become caught up in emotional bondage and to be led astray by our feelings. Our everyday emotions can sometimes feel so strong that they take us by surprise and overwhelm us. They can ensnare and trap us. For some of us, this will seriously impede our walk following Christ. We will stop maturing in the Christian life and not know the true freedom his salvation brings. We might become stuck in what someone referred to as a 'Christian cul-de-sac' as we experience the pull of life's pressures.

The prophet Jeremiah asks, 'The heart is deceitful above all things and beyond cure. Who can understand it?' (Jeremiah 17:9). God can. Obviously he understands it so much better than we do. And through our difficult emotions he is often revealing something amiss about our hearts before him. The problems in our 'horizontal' relationships and interactions with other people are revealing issues in our vertical relationship with God. Our challenge, then, is that rather than listening to our emotions, we need to stop and listen to God – through his word, through prayer and through loving pastoral care.

Helping others effectively

In the church I think we often struggle to effectively help someone who is experiencing difficult emotions. We can be guilty of offering them the grace of God whilst dismissing all other things as if they didn't matter. We can offer words from Scripture such as 'Do not be anxious about anything' (Philippians 4:6) but often do not acknowledge their pain, suffering and deep emotional and spiritual distress. We do not remind them that their identity is in Christ through his death on the cross. Therefore we don't show them how that wonderful biblical truth can be transformed from head knowledge to being truly known in their hearts and lived out in faith and love.

We can also apply the grace of God at the expense of the potential biological component of their emotions. We are complex, embodied souls – biological *and* spiritual – and both dimensions must be acknowledged and connected. There are many illnesses and medications that can present symptoms of emotional difficulties and it is vitally important that these aspects are checked by a GP. Ignoring either the spiritual or biological component of emotional distress can be extremely damaging, for example by encouraging someone to stop taking prescribed medications without first seeking medical guidance.

Perfect emotions

God created us in his image. Through his word we see that he is a thinking God, a God of action and a God of feeling. We also think, act and feel. We see in Jesus, who is fully God and fully human, the perfect demonstration of thinking, behaving and feeling in sinless harmony.

Graham Beynon has written some superb material on emotions. In his fantastic book *Emotions: Living Life in Colour,*[1] he illustrates the sinless emotional life we see in Jesus. Beynon observes that Jesus always felt the right emotion for the event. Not only that but Jesus always experienced the emotion to the right degree for that event.[2] For example, we see Jesus' perfect sorrow through his tears in John 11:35: 'Jesus wept' – the shortest verse in the Bible. Jesus weeps with Mary and others who are mourning the death of Lazarus. In Matthew 21:12–13 we see Jesus experiencing perfect, righteous anger in the temple when he finds people using God's house as a place for buying and selling. But what about us? In this fallen world, as Beynon's diagram illustrates below, we regularly experience either the wrong emotion for the event (for example, points C and D below), or the right emotion for the event but felt to the wrong degree (points A and B).[3] Yet sometimes we experience the correct emotion to the event and to an appropriate level (point E), here because we 'mourn with those who mourn' (Romans 12:15).

wrong emotions

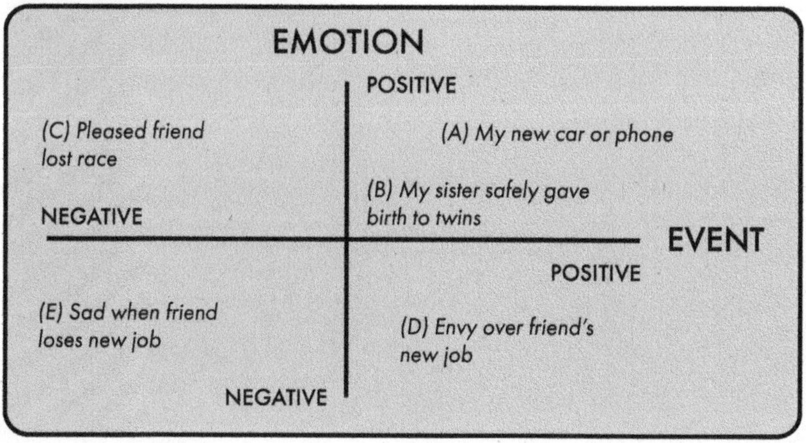

2

Emotions as spiritual smoke alarms

> ***As the heavens are higher than the earth, so are my ways higher than your ways and my thoughts than your thoughts.***
>
> *Isaiah 55:9*

What is going on in a person's heart – their desires – will be reflected outwardly in their lives, through their speech (usually reflecting their thoughts), their emotions and their behaviour. If a person is experiencing a heightened emotional state, you will probably hear them talking like this:

- 'I'm fuming – I can't believe he did that. I've a good mind to go and …'
- 'But it's just such an enormous step to take. How can I know it will work out OK? It doesn't feel safe'
- 'I feel so rubbish about everything. What's the point of it all? I'm so worthless, I want to just give up'

If you then ask them about the situation, they will almost certainly respond not only by describing how they feel – 'I'm so mad'; 'I'm really anxious'; 'I'm worthless' – but also by identifying the cause of this feeling as an external situation:

- 'If she hadn't spoken to me that way I wouldn't have blown my top the way I did'
- 'As soon as I get home the kids start playing up. They just make me lose it – I'm never like this with my colleagues'

We tend to assume that the difficult emotions we experience are a product of the circumstances we face, whether those circumstances are good or bad. Yet whilst the situation is certainly highly significant, it doesn't determine our response. Our emotional reaction comes from us – our whole being – including aspects of which we are generally completely unaware. We will look at these in this chapter.

Ultimately, though, as I have mentioned before, the outer emotion we experience is like a spiritual smoke alarm that is alerting us to a problem of spiritual origins. The emotional difficulties we encounter in our horizontal relationships with other people are a reflection of issues in our vertical relationship with God. They are determined by the loyalties of our heart and what we worship. The issue we need to address is how do we start to decipher the heart of emotions in a way that is meaningful, helpful and, most importantly, biblical?

The 'care of souls'

Traditionally the church has been regarded as the primary source for the care of our souls, including our emotional difficulties. If someone is in the grip of anger, depression or anxiety it undoubtedly affects their walk with Christ, and their awareness of God being with them is often compromised. They need loving pastoral care, discipling them therapeutically to reorient them back towards God. This is true even if they are not explicitly asking for help, as sometimes those who are most in need never ask.

But I wonder if the care of souls has become far less of a priority for our churches in recent decades. Increasing threats and hostility towards the gospel has (quite rightly) increased the focus on evangelism and apologetics – vital areas for the furtherance of the gospel and salvation of the lost. However, I believe that in some cases the church has become overly focused on these areas at the expense of caring for individuals. The result is that those in the church experiencing emotional difficulties no longer look to the church for help. In fact, they may often hide it – perhaps fearing chastisement or judgement by others, or else fearing they are not actually a Christian at all.

The result is that they seek help from secular therapies instead, perhaps with the active encouragement of godly church leaders. Yet in doing so they are intentionally separating out the emotional from the spiritual, compartmentalising them, which can lead to enormous inner tension and spiritual attack. The doctrine of the sufficiency of Scripture tells us that *everything* we need to face life living in his strength in order to serve him is contained in his word – and that includes helping those suffering emotional difficulties.

Perhaps part of the reason many church leaders are reluctant to do so is because they feel fearful or ill-equipped to help people with emotional disorders. Others maybe disagree with 'therapeutic discipleship' and the seeming mix of psychology and Scripture. But the Greek word for therapy, *therapeia*, simply means showing care, attention and healing to those in need of help. Whilst there are clearly some extreme cases of emotional disorder that require very specific specialist intervention, in most cases the church can provide a huge amount of important care. If someone is under the care of their GP, the church can help sensitively alongside that care – and in my experience most GPs are extremely grateful for the support the church can bring to someone struggling. Nor is the church's role just limited to pastoral care teams or senior church leadership – every believer can draw alongside those who are struggling. Such a person needs not only prayer and support in practical ways – for example, meals, lifts and childcare – but also help connecting their life struggles directly to Scripture so as to reorient their hearts towards God in a meaningful way.

Cognitive behavioural therapy

One of the most popular secular therapies in Western society today is cognitive behavioural therapy (CBT). If Christians visit their GP presenting with emotional difficulties such as anxiety, burnout, depression or anger, they are likely to be referred for CBT. At a basic level this works on the premise of: 'What I think affects what I feel, which affects what I do.' To elaborate, the way our senses perceive an event causes our *thoughts*. These thoughts generate an inner *physiological* response and this creates an *emotional* response to the event. This in turn triggers our outer *behavioural* responses. It is for this reason that two people can witness the same event and respond entirely differently to it. The sequence also happens very quickly. Most people will be unaware of the thought processes. All they will perceive is the emotions, which they see as a product of their external circumstances.

Let me illustrate with an example. If a spider lands amongst a group of people in the middle of the floor, it usually generates a mixture of (sometimes extreme) emotions that result in different behaviour. Some individuals may look uneasy. Some may even flee the room. Others may be interested and pick up the spider to examine it or simply pop it in a cup to move it outdoors. What has triggered these differing behavioural responses? In CBT terms it is each person's thoughts. Their perceptions create a mental filter that elicits their emotional and behavioural response.

Those who are picking up the spider and examining it may be thinking, 'Wow – look how unique its markings are, and at the hairs on its legs.' Their internal response is one of heightened interest and emotionally they feel excited. Their resulting behaviour is inquisitive.

Those who are leaping up onto the table and screaming may be thinking, 'Aargh ... it's *huge*! It's just like that one I saw bite someone on TV, and his arm turned *black* before he *died*!!' Their internal response has activated them to 'flight' mode. As a result they are feeling fearful. Their resulting behaviour is one of escape – as quickly as possible.

Those who catch it in a cup may be thinking, 'Oh honestly, what a fuss. Let's pop it outside and get on with our game of Monopoly!' Their internal response has equipped them to 'fight' mode. Emotionally they are feeling highly irritated. Behaviourally they act to remove whatever is getting in the way of what they want.

Looking at this scenario with the spider shows, from a basic CBT perspective, how different emotions happen. When such emotions are experienced, the memory which is created from that event not only records the event but also the unpleasant feelings associated with it. These feelings may then be triggered in subsequent similar events, for example in a phobic response.

The spider example therefore suggests that to change our feelings and behaviour, we must first change our distorted thinking. By identifying unhelpful thinking patterns (known as cognitive distortions) and reconstructing them, we will feel better emotionally. This approach has become increasingly popular in helping people to manage a range of problems, such as anxiety, depression and anger. The diagram below illustrates how thoughts, biology (particularly our physiology), emotions and behaviour are interconnected as we respond to different situations:

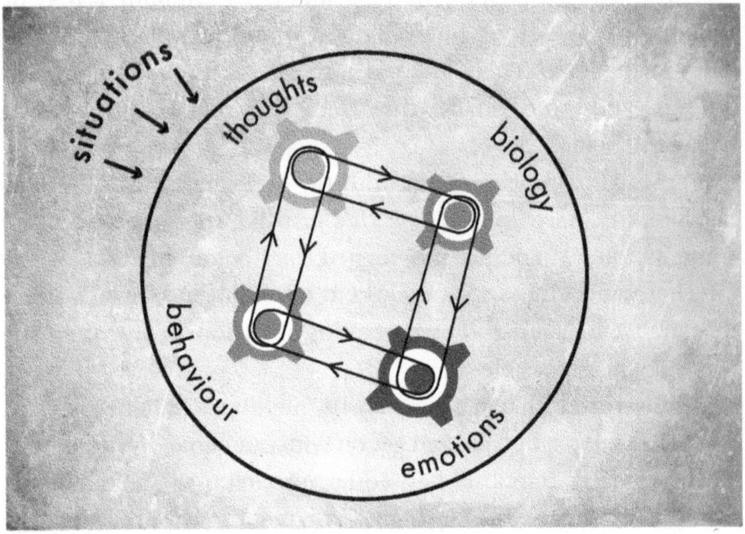

It is of course more complicated than the basic description I have presented here. However, the essence of the cognitive behavioural model comes from the premise that *events in themselves don't cause us emotional disturbance – our thoughts about them do.* Therefore, CBT aims to stop and alter unhelpful thinking styles that can spiral rapidly down into a pattern of negative physical, behavioural and emotional disturbance.

It is effective

CBT has undoubtedly helped many struggling people to cope better with their crippling emotional problems. I too have personal experience of its efficacy. I undertook a basic form of CBT a number of years ago because I was desperate to try to overcome my severe phobia of snakes so as not to influence my children to fear them. Gradually I intentionally educated myself about snakes to alter my thoughts. I also frequently exposed myself to pictures and TV programmes about them. As my heightened physiological state about snakes diminished, my fear subsided. I was delighted when, a few years ago, I stroked 'Horace the python' at a zoo – and can honestly say I enjoyed connecting with part of God's amazing creation.

Empirically we know from our own experiences of emotions, as well as from our observations of others, that the CBT model makes sense: thoughts, biology and behaviours are all undoubtedly experienced in the complexity of the emotional 'package'. For example, when someone is angry, their thinking is clearly distorted and doesn't accurately reflect the reality of the situation. Their physical demeanour certainly illustrates the extent of their pent-up aggression. So too does their yelling at the other person express their dissatisfaction behaviourally. CBT reflects the reality of emotional life!

CBT has other very positive aspects:

- It is a well-established therapy performed by wonderfully caring and compassionate people who dedicate many years to difficult training to help others in their brokenness
- It is an immensely pragmatic, forward-looking, solution-focused approach
- It is logical, easy to use and easy for the recipient to understand
- It has high efficacy, often bringing about positive change in a relatively short period

Is it biblical?

Yet we need to ask whether the CBT model is biblical. Proverbs 3:21 urges, 'do not let wisdom and understanding out of your sight'. As a Christian psychologist, I have therefore considered whether the cognitive behavioural model can bring additional help in discipleship and pastoral care with struggling Christians.

In all areas of life, not just when assessing psychological models, believers face a danger of drifting into one of two camps. The first is to blindly follow something of the world that appears good, without asking whether it is biblical. The second is to simply dismiss those things of the world as having no use in pastoral care work because they are secular in origin. Instead, we can cautiously take what is good and works from secular models – provided they are biblically compatible – and use them wisely, sensitively and effectively in ministry under the primacy of Scripture. Whilst sometimes the two cannot be reconciled, I feel CBT does fit very well, in the most part, with biblical teaching.

For example, it reconciles well, first of all, to the instruction in the Bible that as Christians we should use our minds (our thoughts). Romans 12:2 urges us to 'be transformed by the renewing of your mind'. Similarly, in Acts 17 we see in the apostle Paul *reasoning* with Jews and Gentiles (vv. 1–4), and with Epicurean and Stoic philosophers (vv. 16–34). Whilst of course we must clearly acknowledge the work of the Holy Spirit in this transformation process, these latter passages do illustrate that as we think differently, our beliefs change. Acts 17:34 tells us that after they had listened to Paul's arguments and teaching, 'Some of the people became followers … and believed.'

Once our thoughts are changed, our emotional response is affected too. When we become Christians, we experience peace, as verses such as Romans 15:13 describe: 'May the God of hope fill you with all joy and peace as you trust in him, so that you may overflow with hope by the power of the Holy Spirit.' We love God for what he has done for us through Jesus' death on the cross, rather than feeling hostile or ambivalent towards him. Such a change in our emotions has an impact on our behaviour. We repent of our previous way of living, turning away from wrong and unhelpful behaviours to better ones. The Bible is full of examples of people who have changed their behaviour because of a change in their thinking, such as that of the apostle Paul himself but also ordinary people like the jailer we read of in Acts 16:16–40.

Therefore, I believe that there are significantly helpful parts to CBT that are biblically compatible and can be of great benefit in helping address difficult emotions within a pastoral care setting. If you are struggling emotionally and your GP has referred you for CBT, please go. And if you are currently undergoing CBT, please continue. It will help you.

However, I also have some concerns regarding how, in places, CBT deviates from the authority of Scripture. It is important to address these points both so that believers can look at a situation through a biblical lens and to better equip those discipling them to address the inevitable spiritual component.

I am aware that considering a dry, theoretical view of the basic CBT model is a stark contrast to the practical day-to-day application of dedicated practitioners – both secular and believing. However, David Powlison has challenged my thinking in this area enormously, for which I am extremely grateful, suggesting that CBT veers from biblical teaching in six main areas.[1]

1. Its passive nature

The sequential and progressive nature of the CBT model, as illustrated in the diagram on page 30, shows: distorted thinking = physiological arousal = emotion = behaviour. Yet this seemingly passive view of emotion – where they are derived from thoughts – does not seem to be in synergy with the amazing array and astonishing depth of the emotions addressed in the Bible. Our Creator God displays a full range of emotions, and we do too as we bear his image. Our emotions' origins and purpose is far more than faulty thinking.

2. The relevance of suffering and emotions

In Scripture the acknowledgement of the emotional turmoil experienced due to agonising suffering, and crucially God's purposes in that suffering, extends far beyond the need to change distorted thinking patterns. We only need glance through the psalms to get a sense of the impact of suffering and its associated emotions and to see the importance God attaches to this. No suffering or expressed emotion is out of his control or purposes for our lives.

3. The direction of thoughts

As image bearers of the triune God, we were created to exist in community – to be in relationship with others and ultimately with God. But CBT advocates the need for autonomous, internal self-talk in order to alter distorted thinking patterns. There is undoubtedly a place for this, but the Christian thought life is intended to be fundamentally relational. Our dialogue should be predominantly externally focused, looking towards our living God and his purposes, rather than dwelling on ourselves.

4. Godless solutions

In their work CBT practitioners also look to modify underlying 'silent assumptions' – an individual's belief system and their inherent self-worth – as these in turn affect their thoughts. I absolutely concur with the reality of these belief systems and their cognitive distortions. However, the CBT solution is not gospel-centred. Therefore, as it is godless in origin, it replaces one unhelpful assumption and cognitive distortion with a different but ultimately equally unhelpful one. I will address this point further in a later section concerning changing thoughts.

5. The call to repentance

As David Powlison has remarked, it is interesting to note that the

Stoic philosophers of Acts 17, with whom Paul 'reasoned' (vv. 16–18), were the 'CBT practitioners' of the day. They taught that emotions resulted in destructive errors of judgment and therefore developed cognitive self-control (based on clear and unbiased thinking) as a means of overcoming destructive emotions. Yet what do we see the apostle Paul do? He called them to repentance – to turn away from their philosophies and towards the living God (vv. 22–31).

6. A missing focus

My final but main point of concern is not something that is present or implied in the CBT model, rather something that is missing. That missing component is an intentional look at the desires of the heart. This is crucial in understanding how we experience emotions as part of the complex interaction of body and soul.

What about our hearts?

Consideration of the heart is crucial if pastoral care is to be effective in helping the struggling believer to reorient themselves away from the power of emotions and back towards God. As the light of Scripture is shone into the profound darkness of struggling, it leads to intentional discussions of the heart, so that the Holy Spirit changes us through his transforming, sanctifying grace. Spiritually our heart is our central will and motivator. It generates all our thoughts, emotions and actions.

Luke 6:45 describes the heart's pivotal role in this way: 'A good man brings good things out of the good stored up in his heart, and an evil man brings evil things out of the evil stored up in his heart. For the mouth speaks what the heart is full of.' Our emotions aren't simply triggered by our thoughts and perceptions of an event. Rather, our heart's desires are what flow out into our lives through our thoughts, our physiological responses, our emotional responses and our behaviours. And our heart's desires are determined by our heart's loyalties – what we worship.

If my loyalties are governed by my ambition and desire to be promoted in my job, I will be very 'all or nothing' in my thinking style. I will be physiologically primed to be in 'fight' mode to energise me to push myself forward in my career. Emotionally I will feel angry about those who oppose me by threatening my likelihood for promotion. Behaviourally I may engineer ways of impressing the potential new boss. In summary, all aspects of my being are involved, and they are all directly linked to my heart's loyalties – the pursuit of career which, ultimately, I am worshipping.

Our hearts are dynamic, too easily swinging between God and the competing pulls of the world. When these competing attractions are dominant, we experience a 'gospel eclipse': we stop worshipping God, the giver of all good things, and instead begin to worship our other desires. When we possess what has captured our hearts, we feel good; when we don't or it is threatened, emotional disturbance arises. This emotion is the spiritual smoke alarm that warns us a heart tension exists, but we rarely see it this way. Rather than listening to and investigating the alert, we become consumed and led by our emotion instead.

God is interested in our hearts, the true 'us'. He works in our hearts, speaking through his word and sanctifying us through the work of his Holy Spirit. Whilst it can feel very painful sometimes, this is why I believe that intentionally looking at what is revealed about our hearts in the light of Scripture is a crucial component of both understanding our own negative emotions and supporting others struggling with theirs. Connecting the emotional struggles of life and Scripture in this way is critical in plugging what Paul Tripp and Tim Lane call 'the gospel gap'. In other words, many believers see the work Christ *has* done on the cross and what he *will* do when he returns, but they fail to understand their identity as a child of God *now*. This affects their correct understanding of what Christ is doing in their lives in the *present* moment as they face emotional discomfort.[2]

The 'tbH' model

In my work, I therefore use an adapted version of the cognitive behavioural approach, which I call the 'tbH' model (thoughts, biology and behaviour, and HEART). It addresses all of the ways CBT veers away from Scripture, whilst retaining the helpful components of it when working pastorally with someone in the grip of difficult emotions. It enables those struggling emotionally to be helped to see a couple of important things. First, the emotional difficulty they are experiencing isn't simply a product of 'bad thoughts' – although this is relevant. Second, nor is it simply biological and to be medicated away – whilst there are exceptional rare cases when this is the case. I am not against the wise and cautious use of medication. However, I would be greatly concerned about purely medicating difficult emotions without addressing the struggle at a heart level and in the light of Scripture.

In the tbH model you will notice that the desires of our heart are shown to be central to driving all the components of how we feel: our emotional response, thoughts, biology and behaviour. The will is denoted by the solid black arrows on the diagram below.

Furthermore, the tbH model works on the understanding that it is only a sanctifying heart change through the Holy Spirit that brings about a renewing of the mind. He works through our thoughts, emotions and behaviours to alert us to and alter where our heart's desires have gone astray. This is shown in the diagram by the black dotted lines.

Jesus isn't in the business of facilitating self-help; he is in the business of revealing our hearts and illuminating our disoriented attitudes and desires. When we stop in the midst of struggles to turn and listen to our living God and his promises, our loyalties become reoriented towards him. This brings about transformation in our thoughts, biology, behaviour and emotions. We are progressively changed into the likeness of his Son.

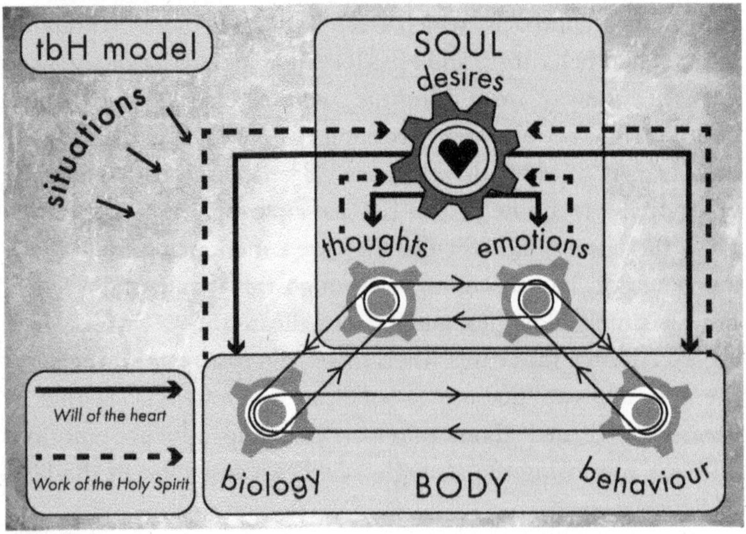

For example, if our spiritual walk is pervaded by repeated arguments, bitterness, grumbling and broken relationships, the tbH model would:

- Reveal something about our *thoughts* and perception of the situation – not just *what* we are thinking incorrectly but *how* we are thinking incorrectly
- Reveal our internal *biology*, which is pumped up in 'fight' mode
- Reveal our *emotions* of anger, which are motivating us to unhelpful action

- Reveal our angry *behaviour*, which exists in many different forms

Together these would all act as a spiritual smoke alarm, revealing the state of our *heart* in the light of Scripture and what we really worship in life. They would also highlight that the anger revealed in our horizontal relationships with others is directly linked to the problem in our vertical relationship with God.

We are inextricably interconnected

We have seen that we are complex combinations of body and soul, separate but also inextricably interconnected. Our thoughts, biology, behaviours and emotions are linked and affect each other, positively and negatively. But the dominant influence on all components is our will flowing from the loyalties of our heart. However, I think it is important to note that there are no sequential stages in the tbH model.

It would not focus, for example, on first changing faulty thoughts about God's character to bring about change in other responses (albeit important to address). Rather, as the tbH approach is used when working with struggling individuals, different components will become more prevalent at specific times: sometimes it will be their spiritual brokenness; sometimes their emotions; sometimes their behaviours; sometimes their biological response; and sometimes their thoughts. The model helps to categorise problem areas more clearly. But all components are communicating vital parts of their struggles and, most importantly, the loyalties of their hearts and their relationship with God. Therefore, all aspects are considered as and when they present themselves.

The tbH approach therefore enables a person's struggle to be framed biblically. Most people are familiar with CBT and can identify with their experience of the different components. Yet tbH helps them to see very clearly the additional link of their heart motives to their unique battle.

We need to see ourselves as Christ does

Those experiencing emotional battles also need to be reminded that the Lord Jesus loves them and is present with them in all their struggles but also that he actively allows their suffering to change them into his likeness. As Paul writes, 'And we know that in all things God works for the good of those who love him, who have been called according to his purpose ... to be conformed to the image of his Son' (Romans 8:28–29). Their struggle isn't hopeless, nor are they a 'weak or failed' Christian. Winston Smith says, rather, their struggle has purpose and their life, however hard that may be, is on a trajectory which is always going somewhere good. This knowledge gives the believer much-needed hope and perspective in the midst of their darkness and struggles.

He states crucially that we must take care not to settle for 'scriptural cognitive re-wiring', whereby we simply think more about Christ: what he has done and who we now are in him.[3] Whilst this is of course very good, it is imperative to help individuals to reorient themselves towards deeper and more meaningful interactions with the living, triune God through faith and repentance shown in changed behaviour. Using tbH as a working model, with Scripture as its foundation, the convicting and redemptive work of the Holy Spirit can be experienced more clearly through the sometimes overwhelming 'noise' of emotions.

The need for hearts pierced by Scripture

Our hearts can only be truly freed from the grip of wrong motives through the penetrating power of Scripture and the work of the Holy Spirit. 2 Timothy 3:16 declares, 'All Scripture is God-breathed and is useful for teaching, rebuking, correcting and training in righteousness'. But the nature of emotional suffering often results in significant 'emotional noise', which can make reading the Bible and praying extremely difficult for the individual. How can Scripture penetrate our hearts if we are unable to concentrate enough to read and meditate on God's word?

We must move away from giving the well-meaning advice of 'just do it': 'you *just* need to go to church more'; 'you *just* need to read your Bible and pray more'; 'you *just* need more fellowship'; or – the ultimate example – 'you *just* need to stop it!' Individuals in the grip of difficult emotions have usually (though not always) really tried to do these things, many times. But the physiological changes that occur during heightened emotions (and the impact of some medications) make them nearly impossible for some to do. And when they can't and are faced with an inevitable spiritual attack, a believer can find themselves in a downward spiritual spiral very quickly. However, if someone can come alongside the person who is struggling using the tbH approach, they can provide 'therapeutic discipleship'. The tbH model allows the different components of the emotional difficulties to be examined, yet always centred on the heart as seen in the light of Scripture.

I believe that we can all benefit from having a working knowledge of this model. This is true whether we are church leaders or members of pastoral care teams, whether we are experiencing emotional difficulties ourselves or are a believer coming alongside our struggling brothers or sisters in Christ. Of course, it is vital to support and help sufferers through the pain of these emotions in practical ways, but it is also imperative to help them see how Christ shines the beauty of his grace through our brokenness, as he moulds them and changes them to become more like him.

The church can be proactive in considering the various aspects of the tbH model in pastoral care. It can assist those helping others to overcome the separation they might feel between the emotional and spiritual components, as well as to resist the temptation to leave the emotional part to the 'secular experts'. It allows the helper to enter the world of the sufferer, connecting together all that they are experiencing and bringing about meaningful change. What a blessing such an approach is compared to simply placating someone with well-meant but often seemingly empty and misused words of Scripture that leave some feeling greatly misunderstood during their plight.

The universality of emotional suffering

There is no doubt that difficult emotions cause extreme suffering. In my work I'm seeing more and more Christians emotionally crippled in their daily walk with Jesus. Sadly, many are often trying to hide it from church leaders. They fear they might be misunderstood, or they feel ashamed and lack assurance when they do not feel the joy of the Christian life. Yet please be clear, if this is true of you, that there is no shame, nor should you feel there is a division between those who do and do not experience emotional distress. We are all on the same emotional continuum because we all have the same hearts – hearts that are naturally inclined away from God. It doesn't take too great a change of circumstances for someone most would consider emotionally robust to experience significant emotional disturbance.

Matthew 16:24 records for us these words from Jesus: 'Whoever wants to be my disciple must deny themselves and take up their cross and follow me.' The Christian life is tough and there are many struggles ahead, including times of emotional struggles. To deny the reality of this is to deny the reality of being a Christian. I therefore think that it is vital that, amongst our Christian brothers and sisters, we start to be more real about our emotional struggles and less naive regarding the prevalence of it in our churches.

God's mercies in our emotional sufferings

Whilst the Christian life can at times be difficult, the wonderful truth is that through it we experience God's mercies. Consider the following words of the lovely song 'Blessings' by American singer Laura Story. The words perhaps become even more poignant when you learn that she, a young mum of a toddler and baby twins, wrote this soon after her husband had been diagnosed with a brain tumour.

We pray for blessings, we pray for peace
Comfort for family, protection while we sleep
We pray for healing, for prosperity
We pray for Your mighty hand to ease our suffering
All the while, You hear each spoken need
Yet love us way too much to give us lesser things

'Cause what if Your blessings come through raindrops
What if Your healing comes through tears
What if a thousand sleepless nights
Are what it takes to know You're near …

What if my greatest disappointments
Or the aching of this life
Is the revealing of a greater thirst this world can't satisfy
What if trials of this life
The rain, the storms, the hardest nights
Are Your mercies in disguise[4]

As Christians, our natural response to someone suffering emotionally is to pray, asking God to remove whatever is causing distress. And this is a good thing to do. But Isaiah 55:9 tells us, 'As the heavens are higher than the earth, so are my ways higher than your ways and my thoughts than your thoughts.' We have already seen that God's loving plans for us are far beyond our understanding, and the difficult emotions we experience are often God's spiritual smoke alarms. They alert us to the fact that deep down something in life is wrong and needs addressing, both at a practical level and spiritual heart level. As the song says, God showers blessings and his mercies on us during 'the rain, the storms, the hardest nights'. True biblical love involves helping a person to see what God may be using their difficult emotions to reveal about their hearts. This can be hard for the helper and the sufferer, and needs great wisdom and sensitivity, but is a huge blessing in our spiritual walks when done by someone gently. However hard and painful difficult emotions are for us to endure, experiencing them is part of God's loving plan and purpose for us as he transforms us into the likeness of his Son.

3

tbH: It's a heart matter!

For where your treasure is, there your heart will be also.
Luke 12:34

In this chapter we will look at the various components of the tbH model to help us understand better what is happening when we are suffering difficult emotions. An emotional response to an event is not simply a feeling caused by the situation we face. As we've already seen, emotions are connected to our thinking, biology (especially our physiology) and behaviour. But at the centre of all of these components, driving them all, is something vitally important: our heart.

The heart component of emotions

We are complex combinations of body and soul which are intimately interconnected. Our heart – the 'real us' – is our worship centre, and whatever we are devoted to drives everything we do, think and feel. It therefore also follows that what we do, think and feel in our lives is a good indicator of what we truly worship and where our loyalties lie. Generally, a good indicator of what someone truly cares about is what they are drawn towards, talk about and pursue in activities.

My eldest daughter, Sophie, loves animals and is happiest when she is in the presence of something small and furry. It doesn't take much for her to joyfully exclaim, 'Aww, it's *adorable*.' Her words are reflecting her adoration of animals. But more than that, her joyful feelings and exclamations profess her worship of the Creator of all things small and furry!

Of course, the same is also true if we feel bitterness in our hearts, for example about someone. At the mention of *that* person's name, we become verbally critical of them to whoever is around. Again, our words reflect our hearts and what we are worshipping – in this case, our main concern is our perceived wellbeing and we are elevating ourselves to the status of almighty judge over the actions of another. Sadly, unkind words, the rolling of eyes and grumbling has hugely damaged many a Christian's witness for Christ. A preacher at the church I attend once warned Christians not to play the 'G.A.M.E.' – the 'Grumbling And Moaning Eclipse'. This sums up the danger brilliantly, I think. What we may think of as a little bit of grumbling does a huge amount of damage to our Christian witness as we eclipse Christ.

So when we experience a difficult and heightened emotion, all components are involved because they are all directly connected to, and driven by, our heart. Which specific part – emotion, thoughts, biology or behaviour – leads in that experience is not clear biblically. The focus for biblical change can be placed on whichever component is most prominent in the person's experience. Yet all aspects are relevant and must be addressed because all are interconnected.

Tarnished hearts

We have seen, then, that what is reflected in our thoughts, biology, emotions and behaviour flows out from the will of our hearts. Luke 12:34 elaborates on this further by telling us, 'where your treasure is, there your heart will be also'. Sophie has a great love and thankfulness for God's wonderful creation, including all things furry. That 'treasure' in Sophie's heart, the worship of God's creation, is reflected in her thoughts and expressed in her joy and in her words. Yet, alas, we do not always treasure or focus our hearts on the right things.

Paul Mallard, in his brilliant book *Staying Fresh*, explains the heart like this:

The heart is something deeper and more comprehensive than both reason [thoughts] and emotion [feelings]. The heart is the deep inner driving force at the centre of all that we are. It is what steers us and shapes us and determines our decisions. It is your authentic self – the core of your being. It is where all our dreams, our desires and our passions live. The heart is like a spring from which waters flow. If your heart is pure, your thoughts and desires and words and actions will be pure. If the spring is poisoned, then all that flows from it will become toxic. If our heart is unhealthy, it has an impact on everything else – our marriage, our family, our relationships.[1]

Jesus himself says in Mark 7:20–21, 'What comes out of a person is what defiles them. For it is from within, out of a person's heart, that evil thoughts come'. The ultimate question for us has to be: '*why?*' *Why* do we think wrongly? *Why* do we behave wrongly? And *why* do we feel wrongly? It is only when we know why we have responded in a certain way to a particular situation that we can be in a better position to address what happens the next time it arises. And the reason why, as Jeremiah 17:9 tells us, is that our 'heart is deceitful above all things'. Furthermore, as Jesus explains, it is from our deceptive hearts that our sinful nature stems. Our heart, the 'real us' and our perceived but sinful needs, is the source of all our human motivation.

The 'real us'

It is a humbling experience when the 'real us' is revealed to others. I once heard a pastor tell the story of a young, stressed doctor who had worked numerous long shifts. The doctor shouted at a nurse who had asked him a simple question. What's more, unfortunately this was in front of all the patients waiting in the hospital clinic for their appointments. Having realised what he'd done, the doctor looked rather embarrassed as he sheepishly muttered, 'I'm sorry, I don't know what came over me there.' But 'what came over him' was the 'real him'. His sinful nature and his heart motives burst through his usually well-managed facade.

It is often when we are at our lowest points physically and emotionally that our 'true self' – our heart – is laid bare and revealed to others around us. When we let our guard down, our heart motives tend to burst out unexpectedly. If you're anything like me, you'll be at your worst at home and to your loved ones. I sometimes feel that as I step through my front door, I morph into some sort of monster-mum!

Of course, our 'true self' – our heart – which we can often manage to hide from others (and sometimes ourselves) is always on display to God. Psalm 139:7 says, 'Where can I go from your Spirit? Where can I flee from your presence?'

It is for this reason that the ultimate focus must be on the loyalties of our heart, which generates all the other components. The intense 'heat' of external trials which bear down on us are of course significant, but they do not determine our emotional response. This flows internally from the functional beliefs of our heart. Therefore two people can respond to the same situation very differently because they have hearts governed by differing desires.

The cognitive (thinking) component of emotions

Undoubtedly, how we think about an event *does* affect how we feel about an event. If I see a motorbike failing to stop as I step out at a zebra crossing, I think, 'It's going to hit me.' I quite rightly feel frightened and my body equips me very quickly to jump back onto the pavement. This is a good and right fearful response. But we also experience negative fearful reactions. For example, I might spend all weekend introspecting and ruminating about a difficult meeting I have to attend on Monday. I imagine how terrible it is going to be, thinking through all the potential disasters. I become tense and wound up. I might even feel quite ill. I might become so anxious that I look for ways I can get out of the meeting. This is all destructive.

Trusting in the promises of God

It is important to see how looking upwards to God and applying biblical wisdom to our distorted thinking differs from internal positive or more rational self-talk. The latter is dependent on our own strength and our own 'worldly wisdom'.

Cognitive distortion (of ourselves or others)	Example distorted thoughts	Biblical wisdom
All-or-nothing thinking Everything is seen at an extreme, with no middle ground	*'If I'm not going to win, there's not point playing'*	*'Each of you should use whatever gift you have received to serve others, as faithful stewards of God's grace in its various forms.' (1 Peter 4:10)*
Over-generalisation Believing we know future outcomes based on a single event	*'Nothing good ever happens to me; it's always rubbish'*	*'For I know the plans I have for you,' declares the LORD, 'plans to prosper you and not to harm you, plans to give you hope and a future.' (Jeremiah 29:11)*
Mental filtering We focus only on certain types of evidence about the situation or person	*'I always mess it up – what's the point?'*	*'Whatever you do, work at it with all your heart, as working for the Lord, not for human masters, since you know that you will receive an inheritance from the Lord as a reward. It is the Lord Christ you are serving.' (Colossians 3:23–24)*
Mind reading / fortune telling We believe we know what people are thinking / that the worst-case scenario will happen	*'I knew they never really liked me' / 'They've got it in for me at work; it'll cost me the promotion'*	*'"For my thoughts are not your thoughts, neither are your ways my ways," declares the LORD.' (Isaiah 55:8)*
Magnification / minimisation Seeing something out of proportion / reducing its significance	*'I couldn't cope without my husband there to support me' / 'Things just went in my favour with the contract'*	*'I can do all this through him who gives me strength.' (Philippians 4:13)*
Emotional reasoning A situation is evaluated on the basis of how we feel about it	*'I'm so scared. It's because it is dangerous to fly'*	*'For I am the LORD your God who takes hold of your right hand and says to you, Do not fear; I will help you.' (Isaiah 41:13)*
Overly demanding thinking Holding unreasonable expectations in the form of 'should' / 'must' / 'ought' / 'never'	*'My spouse and I should never argue with each other' / 'He never listens to me – he's such an awful boss'*	*'For all have sinned and fall short of the glory of God' (Romans 3:23)*
Personalisation / blame Blaming ourselves for something that's not our fault / blaming others for something which was our fault	*'My children have done really badly in their exams; it's all my fault – I'm a terrible parent' / 'Where's my phone gone? You must have moved it'*	*'Do not let wisdom and understanding out of your sight' (Proverbs 3:21)*

When we face a difficult situation in our minds, we all have a tendency to adopt unhelpful thinking styles, known as cognitive distortions. This diagram represents the habitual thinking errors we make. No doubt you recognise some in yourself. We usually have a few particular styles to which we resort. My personal weaknesses are those of mental filtering or magnification, specifically around health issues. I can go from having a headache to diagnosing myself with a brain tumour in five minutes flat. This is reduced significantly to two minutes if I wake with a bad headache in the dark of the night!

Fallen hearts, fallen thoughts

We all have fallen hearts that are naturally inclined away from worshipping God and towards worshipping our own desires. As our senses perceive an event, thoughts are generated that are moulded by our heart's desires, the wellspring of all our life. Our fallen hearts cause our thoughts to be fallen too in *how* we think and in *what* we think. And the interconnection between body and soul means that the functional beliefs of our heart cause a destructive pattern of negative cognitive, physical, behavioural, emotional and spiritual disturbance.

Looking at *what* and *how* someone is thinking about an event provides a gateway to restoring a correct outlook. As we gain an insight into what they truly *want* from the situation and *why* they are thinking that way, the heart of the issue is revealed. Yet one of the biggest problems is that generally people are oblivious to what or how they are *thinking* in a difficult situation. They are far more able to articulate the emotion they are feeling than to articulate their thoughts or inner heart motives. But just as God reveals his thoughts, desires and plans to us through his words, so do we. As the apostle Paul demonstrates in Romans 10:10: 'For it is with your heart you believe and are justified, and it is with your mouth that you profess your faith and are saved.' Our words reflect our hearts. Therefore, if we listen to someone's spoken struggles, with gentle but intentional questioning, we can gain some understanding of their heart.

Many, including those who are struggling, dispute this understanding that fallen hearts and thoughts always lead to a destructive emotional and behavioural pattern. However, it is worth considering the many compelling stories of Christian martyrs who knew they faced impending death yet did not run. Whatever their thoughts, for example their sadness at leaving loved ones, they also knew they would soon be in heaven. Therefore, despite their torture, emotionally they perhaps felt peace knowing that they were glorifying their Lord and Saviour. Thoughts, emotions, biology and behaviour *are* determined by the loyalties of our heart. And when those loyalties are oriented firmly towards Christ, believing that 'to live is Christ and to die is gain' (Philippians 1:21), anything is possible. Trends are 'bucked'. Christians don't feel, think or behave the way the world does.

Changed thinking is vital

Clearly we need to address what something makes us *think*. There is *always* another way of seeing an issue, even if at times it is really hard to discern any other viewpoint. This is well illustrated by the famous optical illusion below. What can you see? The young lady or an elderly lady?

Usually people see one lady very clearly and can't see the other at all. In a similar way, we can get stuck on seeing something only in a certain way because the functional beliefs of our heart act as a filter. But when someone lovingly challenges us and shows us another way to look at the situation, our thoughts and understanding change. If I traced with my finger the image of the lady you *can't* currently see, the picture would change suddenly for you. Likewise, our thinking could experience a 'lightbulb moment' of clarity when someone shows us our heart and erroneous thoughts about the situation, about ourselves, about others and about God. Instead of looking around and seeing only problems, we need to remember that God only sees parts outplaying in his perfect plans for us to become more like Jesus.

This change in perception and understanding is illustrated in the account of the empty tomb in John 20:3–8:

So Peter and the other disciple started for the tomb. Both were running, but the other disciple outran Peter and reached the tomb first. He bent over and ***looked*** *in at the strips of linen lying there but did not go in. Then Simon Peter came along behind him and went straight into the tomb. He* ***saw*** *the strips of linen lying there, as well as the cloth that had been wrapped around Jesus' head. The cloth was still lying in its place, separate from the linen. Finally the other disciple, who had reached the tomb first, also went inside. He* ***saw and believed*** *(my emphasis).*

It is even more striking in the original Greek, where each expression regarding looking reflects a new and different level of understanding, leading to their thoughts about Christ being altered.

Real change?

Many people seeking help for emotional disturbance will experience 'all-or-nothing thinking'. Pessimistically, this may involve thought such as, 'I knew I was rubbish. I didn't get the promotion. I'm an utter failure.' A way of addressing this in CBT terms would be to encourage more realistic or optimistic thinking about the situation and ourselves, and this does help. For example, a realistic thought might be: 'Whatever the interviewers supposed, I know I could have learned to do the job.' Alternatively, an optimistic thought could be: 'I know I would have been better than John, who got the promotion. Just watch: he will be a disaster and they'll see the mistake they made in not choosing me!'.

But can you see what has occurred? Whilst cognitive change has happened, and the person may well feel better, it is based on the person's own strength and ability to engage in positive self-talk and thinking. Undoubtedly this does help and there is a place for it. Yet in doing so they have really established new unhelpful thinking styles, based on a more elevated view of themselves. They may also be completely inaccurate. Perhaps the person genuinely was a disaster at the interview and have resisted constructive feedback regarding their sub-standard performance for years!

Redemptive change

Redemptive change occurs when our altered thoughts are based on a more accurate understanding of ourselves based on who we are in Christ. This is not simply a more optimistic or rational view of ourselves to counteract the pessimistic cognitive distortions.

By being aware of what can go wrong in our thinking we can helpfully decipher the potential dangers of our heart. In love, we can help others to openly and honestly ask what their thoughts and emotions are revealing about the functional beliefs and desires of their heart. These can then be framed in the light of appropriate Scripture to encourage active turning towards and honest dialogue with the living God, asking to be shown the situation through his eyes.

For example, we might understand that God has knit us together in our mother's womb (Psalm 139:13–14) and therefore be reassured that we are special to God. Or we might ponder, 'How can I use the gift's God has given me to the best of my ability so as to put into practise Colossians 3:23: "Whatever you do, work at it with all your heart, as working for the Lord"?' Turning to God and biblical wisdom brings about changed thoughts. Sanctifying change happens not when we counteract pessimistic thinking styles with realistic or optimistic self-talk. Nor does it happen when we simply think about God more or try to give our cognitive rewiring the appearance of a scriptural base. Changed thinking must translate into faith in action, as we are told in James 2:14: 'What good is it, my brothers and sisters, if someone claims to have faith but has no deeds? Can such faith save them?' Through the power of the Holy Spirit, reoriented Christ-centred thinking connects head knowledge to the heart and turns faith into action. It steps out in trust, behaving differently based on God's promises to us in the security of our identity in Christ.

The biological component of emotions

When we experience an emotion, other components are involved. They impact each other but are all ultimately independently triggered by the orientation of our heart. Let's reconsider the spider example I used in the previous chapter. (Sorry to anyone reading this who struggles with spiders!) On seeing a spider land in the room, we might feel utter terror, as many do. Our inner heart affects our outer body, priming it for action: to run away.

We can better understand how the perception of the spider has activated responses in the body by looking at exactly what is happening physiologically. There is far more to it than this but here is a very basic description. The cerebral cortex processes information received from our senses about the spider. This sends information to the anterior hypothalamus, which is a section of the brain responsible for certain metabolic processes and the production of many of the body's essential neurohormones. The hypothalamus in turn sends messages to the automatic nervous system (ANS), which controls the heart, lungs, blood vessels, stomach and glands. The ANS then responds to the received information depending on whether it is perceived as a threat or not, and this determines which component of the ANS becomes more dominant – the parasympathetic nervous system (PNS) if it is a non-stressful situation, for which a relaxed equilibrium can be maintained; or the sympathetic nervous system (SNS) if action is required.

So, if the perception of the spider is considered a threat, *whether that threat is real or imagined*, the sympathetic nervous system produces neurotransmitters to prepare the body's 'flight' or 'fight' response to deal with the spider. This creates the necessary physiological adjustments to the bodily organs. If the threat is perceived as needing a 'fight' (aggressive) response, hormones prepare the body to feel pumped up and full of energy, with an individual feeling, 'I'm in control.' Conversely, if the threat is perceived as needing a 'flight' (fear) response, hormones prepare the body for flight, creating a feeling of being 'out of control' together with perhaps a thudding heart and a strong desire to flee.

We will all have experienced times when a dominant SNS has resulted in varying physiological changes to enable us to deal with a particular situation. For example, at stressful times a doctor may tell us we have elevated blood pressure. This is caused by a quickening in our heart rate to increase oxygen flow to our muscles. Times of stress often produce cold, clammy hands because body temperature in our extremities is quickly reduced as blood is directed towards vital organs. A 'butterflies' sensation (sometimes resulting in sudden vomiting or diarrhoea) is caused by a decrease in movement in the gut muscles and digestive activity as blood supply is diverted elsewhere. Other more imperceptible changes that take place include dilated leg and arm muscles (in preparation for 'flight' or 'fight'); quicker breathing to increase the air flow available; liver and fat tissues mobilising sugar and fats around the body for increased energy; and the blood becoming more able to clot in case of injury.

If the stress response, resulting in feeling anxious or angry, is experienced regularly, this internal response becomes chronic. The anterior hypothalamus activates the pituitary-adrenal cortex system, which kicks into action and produces cortisol (to regulate sugars and fats into the system), increases blood pressure and blood sugars, and suppresses pain, inflammation and immunity. However, high levels of cortisol in the long term can result in burnout or breakdown for the individual. It also contributes to many long-term serious health conditions. This is partly due to the suppressed immunity effect – meaning that you will often get lots of coughs and colds. But it also significantly increases the risk of hypertension and cardiovascular disease as the continuous releases of fats into the blood stick to walls of the veins, thus causing narrowing of the arteries. Eventually these tend to drop off, but this then increases the risk of clots and embolisms.

Whilst we have been looking above at the stress response in the context of anger and anxiety, to an extent similar physiological sensations can be a response to a number of different positive *and* negative emotional arousal states. However, when linked to negative emotional arousal, these bodily sensations have a tendency to last longer and have a higher degree of intensity and unpleasantness. As a result, they will feel far harder to live with and potentially will become more debilitating, significantly affecting our ability to carry out normal everyday 'life'. It also dramatically impacts our walk following Christ, hindering us from experiencing the blessing and fullness of living out our new identity in Christ.

In Luke's Gospel we see the Lord Jesus suffering a distressing physiological response to an intense situation. As he prays in the garden of Gethsemane, preparing himself for the impending cross of Calvary, we witness his agony. He faces the reality of spiritual separation from his beloved heavenly Father and the agony of bearing his wrath because of our sins, and we're told that Jesus' 'sweat was like drops of blood' (Luke 22:44). Hematidrosis (where sweat contains blood) is a rare but very real physiological response to extreme emotional or physical anguish. The sweat glands, which are surrounded by tiny blood vessels, constrict and then dilate to the point of rupture, causing the blood to mix with sweat in the glands. Jesus knew he faced unimaginable pain and death, in his body and soul. Physiologically, he showed the effects of this certain knowledge. And yet – unlike our normal human reaction – behaviourally he was silent and obedient, like a lamb to the slaughter.

The behavioural component of emotions

The way we think and feel can affect how we behave, and behaviour can be either helpful or unhelpful in a situation. Thus, negative thoughts and emotions can contribute to adverse behavioural patterns.

Often our behavioural solution *is* the problem! It might seem that some of our behaviour, such as avoidance or being controlling, is a good way of responding because they work – in the short term. So, for example, if you have a panic attack on a tube train and therefore after that avoid going on tubes, in the short term your action plan helps – you don't have another panic attack. Further problems arise, though, if your panic attacks escalate, such as occurring on buses too. Now you are locked in a downward spiral of destructive thoughts and behaviour.

Alternatively, think of a scenario in church. Maybe someone says something that hurts you. Your solution may be to avoid that person because this feels easiest – you are not, for example, having to confront it. Yet before you know it, you could be avoiding not just the same house group you are in but also avoiding fellowship meals together and then the Sunday morning service too.

Behavioural response also includes 'action tendencies', which are strong desires to behave in a particular way, even if you don't actually physically do so. For example, I might feel very angry at someone. I don't go up to them and yell at them but over and over in my mind I replay the thoughts and fantasise about giving them a 'piece of my mind'.

Remember, though, that all components, including our behaviour, are ultimately driven by the desires of our heart. For example, if we are driven by a heart that is motived by acceptance from others rather than acceptance from God, our behaviour is affected detrimentally. We may compromise on what we know to be morally right in a relationship to please that person rather than God – here our fallen behaviour is working on a horizontal level. Then we may stop praying, reading God's word or listening to others preaching from it so we can ignore this fact and sit more comfortably with it. The will of our hearts has had a direct impact on our vertical relationship with God.

In Judges 6:36–40 we see Gideon's dominant heart desires affecting his behaviour:

Gideon said to God, 'If you will save Israel by my hand as you have promised – look, I will place a wool fleece on the threshing-floor. If there is dew only on the fleece and all the ground is dry, then I will know that you will save Israel by my hand, as you have said.' And that is what happened. Gideon rose early the next day; he squeezed the fleece and wrung out the dew – a bowlful of water.

Then Gideon said to God, 'Do not be angry with me. Let me make just one more request. Allow me one more test with the fleece, but this time make the fleece dry and let the ground be covered with dew.' That night God did so. Only the fleece was dry; all the ground was covered with dew.

Gideon was in the grip of fear. He knew what he had to do: obey God by leading Israel in battle out of Midian's hand (Judges 6:11–14). But he was terrified of the Midianites who for so long had oppressed Israel and therefore Gideon didn't entirely trust God. The functional beliefs of his heart were screaming of his desire to do things his way instead. His thoughts and internal physiology were probably in a panicked state. As he sought control, he looked for reassurance from what was essentially a ritualistic process, a bit like touching wood or throwing salt over your shoulder. This resulted in the behaviour we see in the verses above: he bargained with God. But just look at God's wonderful grace and mercy towards Gideon: God mercifully helped and strengthened Gideon for the task ahead.

Conflicting pulls

There are so many conflicting voices and pulls on our souls from society today and they greatly impact our walk following Christ. Considering these areas of thinking, biology and behaviour can help us to see those pulls and distractions more clearly. Techniques such as CBT have been proven to be highly effective in the therapy room – they categorically can and do help. But God has much greater things planned for us. He desires us to become more like his Son. This requires submitting our hearts to him, which is why the heart component of tbH – where it is clearly seem to drive all the others – is so important. Instead of being led by our powerful emotions and overcome by their 'noise', we can see the emotion as a mirror of our heart. We then can ask, 'What do I really want out of this situation? What is driving my heart? What are my functional beliefs? Where do my true loyalties lie? Are they with God or with something or someone else?'

Through gaining an awareness of what is being revealed about our heart during emotional difficulties, and framing the situation biblically, we can be more responsive to God's word. This pierces our hearts and breaks down our unhelpful heart motives. As we turn and converse with God, we see him more clearly at work in us through our struggle. As we step out in faith through action, we experience the freedom of his restorative grace.

4

Suffering: The sneers, the fears and the tears

As water reflects the face, so one's life reflects the heart.
Proverbs 27:19

In the last chapter we looked at the different components of the tbH model. In this chapter I'd like to introduce a number of commonly experienced everyday emotions that sometimes have debilitating effects in our Christian walk. I'd like us to consider what the components of the tbH model look like when applied directly to these emotions. As we are a complex combination of body *and* soul, when we are struggling emotionally, there is *always* a spiritual component. This means we *must* address our heart motives. Simply medicating away uncomfortable emotions or altering unhelpful thoughts and destructive behaviours without addressing the heart of emotion is missing out on opportunities to hear God's voice and to grow in our spiritual walk following him. Moreover, we can confront the difficulty in God's strength and from the security we have in our identity in Christ, as 'he gives us more grace' (James 4:6) to do so.

When we consider emotions, they are commonly grouped together. My four cluster names I find it helpful to work with are the '*cheers*', the '*sneers*', the '*fears*' and the '*tears*'. The 'cheers' are those emotions such as joy, peace, contentment and love that we associate with being a Christian and wish we experienced in their fullness all the time. Unfortunately, we are more likely to experience, at least at times, the more uncomfortable and difficult emotional clusters, so this is what I would like to focus on.

When a believer frequently experiences these more testing emotional clusters, they can doubt their salvation, asking, 'How can I be a Christian if I feel this way?' Yet we can be encouraged that God is at work through such difficult emotions. Hebrews 12:7 tells us, 'Endure hardship as discipline; God is treating you as his children. For what children are not disciplined by their father?' Difficult emotions are extremely hard to bear, but God lovingly allows us to experience that hardship to reveal those areas which are pulling us away from fully worshipping him. There is hope: he is speaking into our hearts and pouring his abundant grace onto us.

The uncomfortable clusters

My three categories for those emotions we find difficult can be broken down further as follows:

- The 'sneers' are those emotions directed at and against people. They include irritation, frustration, anger, contempt, pride, envy, spite, jealousy, hatred, loathing, fury, resentment and bitterness
- The 'fears' are those emotions that take us away from people. They are emotions rooted in future-oriented thinking and include dread, panic, distress, nervousness, unease, helplessness, anxiety, feeling overwhelmed, worry and insecurity
- The 'tears' are those emotions rooted in loss that take us into ourselves. They include disappointment, hurt, despair,

guilt, alienation, isolation, hopelessness, unhappiness, lack of joy, rejection, misery and depression

Emotions are complex and it is very common to experience a number of different emotions at the same time. Sometimes what we feel won't neatly fit into the clusters I have suggested here. For example, panic or hurt can often trigger a defensive angry response. At times our son, James, has very surprising outward responses to an event and it has taken my husband, Richard, and me many years to try to discern and understand what he is thinking, feeling and being motivated by, based on his behaviour. It is blurry and complicated! But the clusters do act as helpful categories for looking at some emotions in a practical way. The emotional themes they represent are also very helpful in connecting thematic Scripture to the issues that person is facing in their life in a more meaningful way.

Seeing life through unhelpful mental filters

We all approach life through various filters. At this point it would be helpful for you to assess those that influence you, so I would like you to fill out the emotions questionnaire in Appendix 1 at the back of this book. Then look at your total scores for the different 'F', 'S' and 'T' groups I have indicated.

I would imagine that some of you have scores quite high on 'F'. This suggests that you will tend to view the events in your life through a filter of fear. You are therefore likely to suffer quite a lot of worry and anxiety. If your highest score is 'S', the sneer emotions filter how you view events. You are likely to suffer a lot of bitterness and irritation in your relationships. Finally, if 'T' is your highest score, you see events through a sadness or loss filter. You are likely to experience a lot of insecurity, hopelessness and possibly even depression in your life. Although it is rather a rough and ready questionnaire, it serves a useful practical purpose here in indicating your most likely filters.

I have already mentioned that as experiences occur in life, we can come to see ourselves as being defined by them. Our memories of them are stored in groups with similar experiences (called schemata) as well as the emotions attached to them. Thus mental filters build up and these affect the way we see subsequent but similar events that happen in our lives. For example, someone who has had many experiences of extreme frustration as a child may as an adult see everything through a frustrated ('sneer') filter. Their response to virtually everything may be bitterness and anger. Alternatively, someone who has sadly experienced an aggressive parent in childhood may see everything through a lens of fear, even towards those things that aren't considered fearful at all by others. Yet these filters not only affect how we perceive events in our life; they affect how we see ourselves and our identity. They can also affect how we see God, who gives us our identity.

Identifying with emotional suffering

The life of someone experiencing difficult emotions is hard and involves a great deal of suffering. Paul Tripp, in his fantastic book *Instruments in the Redeemer's Hands*,[1] suggests that identifying the person needing support as a *sufferer* helps them in a number of ways that are vital in aiding recovery, these being:

- It allows them to more readily identify with the many parts of Scripture that address suffering
- It highlights the temporary nature of their suffering, which will usually last only a short period in this life but certainly will not exist in the next
- It helps prevent them from identifying themselves as a 'victim', or as someone who is 'depressed', 'anxious' or

'angry'. Whilst these emotions may be a large component of their lives at this moment, their true identity is in Christ – we are a new creation in him
- It highlights the fact that they have responsibility to help themselves. If we feel cold, we can put a jumper on to warm up. Likewise, it is crucial that responsibility for change is embraced in emotional suffering. No-one, however loving and compassionate, can do that for them

I think this is all invaluable advice. We need to empathise with those who suffer due to their difficult emotions but also point them to these scriptural truths, encouraging them to change and not to identify themselves as a victim of their (sometimes devastating) circumstances. 2 Corinthians 5:17 tells us, 'Therefore, if anyone is in Christ, the new creation has come: the old has gone, the new is here!' As a believer, their identity is as a new creation in Christ, despite their suffering. Their suffering is not their identity.

Putting emotional suffering in its proper place

It's important to know, though, that suffering difficult emotions isn't a 'bad thing' that should be avoided at all costs. In fact, it is psychologically damaging to actively avoid feeling difficult emotions. We are told in the Bible: 'Rejoice with those who rejoice; mourn with those who mourn' (Romans 12:15), so there is clearly a right time for experiencing difficult emotions.

Yet there is also a right *way* to experience situations and emotions. Emotional resilience is defined psychologically in Michael Neenan's book *Developing Resilience*[2] as an individual's ability to *properly* adapt to difficulties and adversity, which is not to be mistaken for heroic stoicism. This involves being able to find positive meaning from misfortune and difficulties. People who are able to do this usually come out of the other side of emotional difficulty emotionally stronger than before. Through a biblical lens, we can help someone to be brought back to see their identity in Christ and the character (and sometimes also the purposes) of God more clearly. However, if positive meaning is not based on biblical truth, we have simply created another problem, albeit based on a more positive view. Biblical wisdom is not about seeing the situation, ourselves and others through rose-tinted spectacles. It is about seeing them accurately, through God's eyes.

Difficult emotions will become problematic when they are felt out of proportion to the situation and when they take the lead in controlling our lives, rather than us submitting to the will of God and trusting him to lead us. Then the self-fulfilling thoughts and behavioural cycle kick in, as does spiritual attack, and we are debilitated. Whenever we are faced with difficult emotions, our hearts are faced with a choice: do we turn towards God or away from him? Do we do things his way or our way? When we are led by our emotions, we have chosen the latter.

For this reason, over the next few chapters we will spend a little bit of time looking at each of the three emotional clusters, applying the tbH model of thoughts, behaviour and heart to them. We will examine what they feel like, what thoughts they might prompt and how they can cause us to behave. Most importantly, we will also consider what the emotional mirror might be reflecting about our hearts under the spotlight of Scripture.

Just imagine how much more God's kingdom would be built in our churches if we became more honest and intentional about our hearts and submitted our heart motives over to him. Wouldn't it be wonderful to feel secure in our identities in Christ and serve him, knowing his peace and freedom from the grip of difficult emotions? We can, so please do read on.

5
The sneers

Do not be quickly provoked in your spirit, for anger resides in the lap of fools.

Ecclesiastes 7:9

The first emotional cluster we will look at is the 'sneers'. These are the angry emotions directed at and against people. As previously mentioned, the cluster includes irritation, frustration, contempt, pride, envy, spite, jealousy, hatred, loathing, fury, resentment and bitterness. These are all derivatives of anger. The festering bitterness and grumbling about others plus the rolls of the eyes, tuts and sighs are certainly common to many. Sadly, they are present too much in our churches.

We will focus on two common but debilitating sneers – anger and a bitter spirit. We will apply the tbH model to them, consider a case study and finally apply the tbH model to ourselves. To remind you, the tbH is the following:

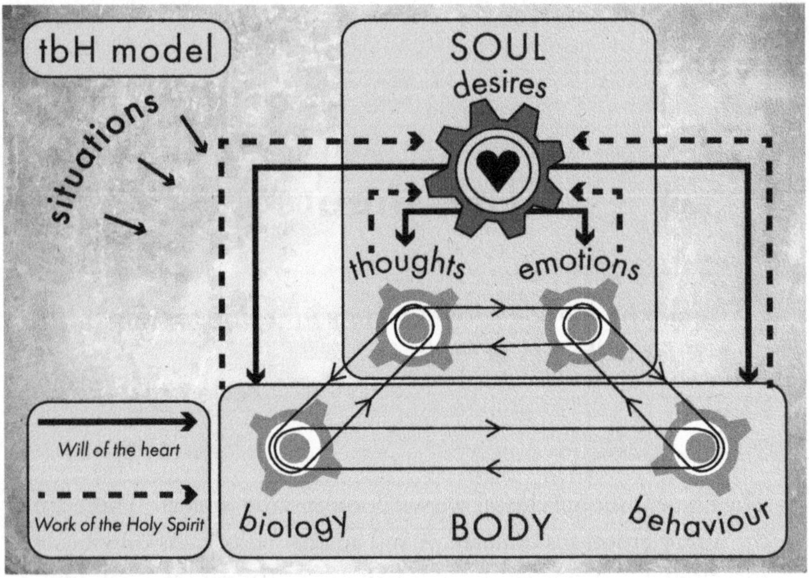

Thoughts

What do we think and how do we think when we are angry? *How* we think is revealed through the typically destructive thought patterns associated with anger and bitterness. They are those thoughts that become far more focused on the 'irritant'. If you look back at the chart of unhelpful thinking styles in chapter 2, cognitive distortions often present include:

- **All-or-nothing thinking:** As we have rigid and extreme attitudes, we may speak to others unhelpfully about a person, in order to support our negative views of them
- **Mental filtering:** We look for specific evidence to support us being right and the other person being wrong. We ruminate on negative events, reflecting on them over and

over in our minds. We may try to look for evidence of malicious intent from others

- **Emotional reasoning:** As we feel a certain way – annoyed – we believe the situation must be viewed that way
- **Overly demanding thinking:** We adopt highly critical and judgemental thinking about others not meeting our standards
- **Blame:** We readily blame others, for example along the lines of: 'They're useless – they always mess everything up whenever they're asked to help'

Biology

All anger or bitterness will produce physiological changes in the body through the nervous system, as I previously outlined in chapter 3, with in these instances it being the 'fight' mechanism that is activated. This biology affects people at different points as we all have different levels of tolerance. But when we do react, our heart rate rises, as does our blood pressure. Our bodies become pumped for action and angry outbursts lie just below the surface waiting for provocation. We can feel 'prickly' simply when the person we feel bitterness towards walks into the room. We feel pent-up with pressure.

Behaviour

Those feeling anger or bitterness may have behavioural tendencies such as seeking revenge, attacking a person verbally, or gossiping, being critical or being judgemental about an individual to all who will listen. We perhaps try to recruit allies against others. We can be demanding or destructive in relationships. We may manipulate others to avoid the person we feel bitter towards. More passive aggressive actions can include sulking or the silent treatment. We might use tuts, audible sighs and rolls of the eyes when speaking of the individual. If bitterness is festering away, we will repeatedly bring up events of the past to remind the individual concerned, or others, about the person's failings. Maybe we just imagine a scene where the person 'finally gets what is coming to them'. These are all outward demonstrations of an active emotion like anger or of what many would consider a more passive emotion such as bitterness of spirit. However, bitterness grows into anger, so don't dismiss the damage festering bitterness does to your spiritual walk and witness for Christ.

Right or wrong anger?

To repeat a previous point I made, it is important to remember that not everything identified in the spectrum of anger can be considered bad or sinful. Ephesians 4:26 tells us, 'In your anger do not sin'. Our natural tendency of course *is* to sin when we are angry, but this verse clearly implies it is possible to be angry *without* sinning. We have a choice. We see Jesus experiencing sinless anger in the temple as he drives out those who had turned God's house into a den of thieves (Matthew 21:12–13). We also know from 1 Corinthians 10:13 that sinning in our anger is not inevitable because the apostle Paul writes, 'God is faithful; he will not let you be tempted beyond what you can bear. But when you are tempted, he will also provide a way out so that you can endure it.'

What is important is our heart motives generating the physiological arousal of anger, and whether we respond sinfully to the arousal. This is most clearly revealed through our words and actions. In order to establish whether our anger is sinful, we need to ask ourselves, for example, do we wish the person well or harm? Do we seek revenge? Do we lash out verbally? Or perhaps do we give someone the cold shoulder or avoid them? If our anger is wrong, there is always the tendency to blame others or blame our circumstances. We might say: '*He* made me do it,' or '*She* drove me crazy and I just exploded,' but it is not correct to blame others in this way. Anger is a response from us and it involves all of our body and soul.

Acting by grace or the flesh?

Powlison makes the wise observation that people will be motivated either by grace or by the flesh.[1] The crux of the matter is that two people can be confronted with the same provocation, which places significant pressure on them both, but the testing situation itself does not determine their response. One can respond biblically, motivated by grace – thus not sinning – whilst the other responds motivated by the flesh and therefore in a sinful way. If our response is motivated by the flesh, through our anger and bitterness many relationships will suffer greatly, including our relationship with God. But make no mistake about this: we, as the perpetrator of the anger, will be suffering too. Living life with bitterness and anger towards others is a miserable place to be.

Before I was converted, I had a real temper. I was more of a thermometer than a thermostat. Unlike a thermostat, which switches off on reaching a certain temperature, I would just boil inside and then explode, yell and throw things. Our backgammon board never recovered after an unfortunate end to a marital board games evening! I am so thankful that through Christ I have been given self-control as a fruit of the Spirit. It is rare these days for my explosions to happen. But it is also true to say that I face a regular battle with an inner rage boiling away inside me. I consistently need to manage it in a way that is God-honouring, and sometimes I fail. Dealing with that internal boiling feeling isn't nice. It is painful to carry, and it is exhausting to manage and deal with it in constructive ways. It is hard to talk about and be honest about before God and with friends. I feel guilty and I feel confused. It can cause me to lack assurance, as Satan accuses me, 'How can you call yourself a Christian if you feel this way and cause others to suffer too?'

Out of the three emotional clusters, the sneers are perhaps the most difficult in which to bring about change. Often the bitter spirit festers and grows slowly. Anger doesn't always involve shouting and aggression – passive anger, sulking or pushing back and away from others is equally as damaging. We don't realise the impact we are having on others. People might be reluctant to speak gently but truthfully to us about the impact of our behaviour in case we become bitter and angry towards them too. In the mind of someone who sees everything through an angry or bitter filter, they truly believe that they are right and everyone else is wrong, including those who are seeking to lovingly point them towards Christ.

Bitter people believe they are justified in the way they are thinking and acting. It is typical to blame the anger on another or the situation. James, though, doesn't hold back from telling us how it really is: 'What causes fights and quarrels among you? Don't they come from your desires that battle within you? You desire but do not have, so you kill. You covet but you cannot get what you want, so you quarrel and fight. You do not have because you do not ask God' (James 4:1–2).

In fact, the sneers are quite effective in the sense that they usually result in the angry or bitter person getting what they want. People tip-toe around cautiously, never quite knowing what to expect from them, or people give in to the sulky cold shoulder treatment to reduce tension. These 'wins' or 'rewards' then reinforce the thoughts and behaviour of those who are angry or bitter. Perhaps we only start to realise the 'common denominator' in all our difficult situations might be us when we notice how many fractured relationships exist with our family, friends and colleagues.

The heart

What we think is a reflection of what our heart worships at that moment and what we want more than we want God. We need to get down to the nitty gritty of the matter: what is *really* going on in the heart? Anger and bitterness point to what is truly important to us: the '*real* us' that only God fully sees – that is until it bubbles over in public. Ed Welch observes very wisely, 'When in doubt, look at what is going on inside you.'[2] The Bible describes this in Proverbs 27:19: 'As water reflects the face, so one's life reflects the heart.' I would summarise the situation as follows:

What is dominating the heart when we are angry or bitter? What is the heart matter? When we look at these emotions through the lens of Scripture, this reveals *a focus on 'me'* as the judge of the situation and a heart of *pride*. My personal rule or standard is violated or is threatened or blocked in some way; there is a perceived transgression against 'me'. My heart of pride puts me and my rules at the centre of everything and above everyone else, *including God*. My resulting behavioural response is to actively punish people, either overtly by yelling at them and cutting them out of my life, or more covertly by gossiping and being critical about them in my speech.

The way we treat others on a horizontal level depicts how we live out the second greatest commandment Jesus gave us: 'Love your neighbour as yourself' (Mark 12:31). This incorporates the last six of the ten commandments given to Moses: honouring parents, not murdering (or even being angry), being faithful to our marriage partner, not stealing, being truthful and not coveting. It also reveals the condition of our hearts and reflects the state of our vertical relationship with God. It represents how we live out the most important commandment Jesus gave us: 'Love the Lord your God with all your heart and with all your soul and with all your mind and with all your strength' (Mark 12:30). This is demonstrated by observing the first four of the ten commandments: worshipping God alone.

The two great commandments that Jesus states are inextricably linked. If we fail to keep the second, we are not honouring the first. This is illustrated perfectly through the experience of anger. When someone thwarts our plans or causes us discomfort or inconvenience in some way, we *want* to punish them and make them suffer. Just consider for a moment how this plays out in an incident of road rage! Yet when we seek to inflict revenge on other believers, think about what we are really doing. Tim Chester brilliantly explains it in this way: we're demanding a second payment for something that has already been paid for in full by Jesus' death on the cross. We are saying that his death wasn't enough and our judgement is better than God's.[3]

It's no longer about us

However, the cross of Christ means that it is no longer about us; it's all about God, his purposes for us and our relationship with him. It is God who has ordained this situation or person into our lives, in this particular way, at this particular time. Our anger at others reflects, deep down, our anger at him and his will for us at that specific point in our lives. It is a rejection of the command in 1 Thessalonians 5:18: 'give thanks in all circumstances; for this is God's will for you in Christ Jesus.' When we have fully understood the cross and our new identity in Christ, our focus is directed at our responsibility for our sin before God, rather than being focused on someone else's wrongdoing. Let God deal with that because his judgement and anger is perfect; ours isn't.

As Tim Chester says, 'Good anger is an emotional response to the right things (sin and injustice) in the right way (controlled and desiring good).'[4] We therefore must examine our heart of pride before God. I have heard David Powlison speak many times of our attitude as, 'My kingdom come, My will be done' – we need to let go of such thinking, and bring these broken and destructive emotions of anger and bitterness to the foot of the cross, where Jesus paid the price in full for us to be washed clean.

I hope the following case study demonstrates this further.

Case study

Tom was thirty-six years old and married with three young children. He and his wife had both become Christians in their late teens and had married a few years later. He had a successful career and managed a large team of professionals. He'd always hoped he would go into Christian ministry but 'things kept getting in the way' and 'God wouldn't open that door'.

When Tom came to see me, he said he was experiencing anxiety due to family and work pressures. Cracks were starting to show in his marriage that he attributed to his wife's increasingly uncooperative behaviour. His eldest son was having a few behavioural problems at school that Tom considered 'unacceptable'. These matters and others dominated his thoughts and attention at home. At work he felt he was the only one really capable of doing the job correctly and with integrity, and considered most others in the office 'imbeciles, incapable of doing what they were paid for'. As a result he was shouldering more and more of the work burden too.

Having established those areas in which he was struggling, we began our sessions working through the components of tbH.

Thoughts / primary cognitive styles

- Overly demanding thinking
- Over-generalisation
- Blame (on others)
- Mental filtering

Biology / physiology

- Pumped up and agitated
- Unable to rest
- Poor sleep
- Tight stomach all the time
- High blood pressure (and taking appropriate medication)
- Heart palpitations (under investigation)

Behaviour

- Explosive tendencies at his wife and children, and increasingly in the office
- Heavily disciplined his children because he thought they would 'just do things to deliberately wind me up, so they needed serious discipline'
- Had stopped going to church because he didn't like the way it was run and the preacher 'just droned on'
- Increasingly avoided social interactions in general because he found everyone annoying
- Highly critical of everyone in his speech – he was right and everyone else was wrong in virtually every area of his life
- Rolled his eyes as he spoke of others and their 'stupidity'
- Spoke of the burdens laid on him as he 'sorted everyone out'

The heart of the matter

The heart of the matter was his *pride*: a belief that his 'rights' had been violated by God and by others. All his thinking was about him and what he believed he deserved. He was bitter towards his wife, who was highly regarded as she served in a ministry role whereas he didn't. He was bitter towards his eldest son, who wasn't succeeding to his desired high personal standard. He was angry at his colleagues, who pushed back at his increasingly demanding managerial style.

Ultimately Tom's heart of worship was himself and his desires, rather than submitting to God's perfect will for his life, and he was angry at God. The 'ministry' he was primarily called to was to be a godly husband and father in his home, and to work as hard as he could as if working for God rather than men. But this wasn't the ministry he wanted or felt he deserved. His 'good wants' of serving in church ministry and having a good marriage and obedient children had turned into 'destructive needs' and were ruling his heart. He felt they were his 'rights', so when anyone, including God, seemed to get in the way, his behavioural response was explosive. He was sitting in his personal judgement over everyone rather than showing the mercy God had shown him.

The next step is of course to apply the same method to our own hearts. Therefore please take the time to prayerfully work through the following questions, identifying those areas where you need to change. Where is God in your situation?

How about you?

Consider the questions below regarding a person or situation about which you are feeling an 'active' anger or a more 'passive' bitterness.

Situation	• What / who made you angry or bitter?
Thoughts	• What did you think?
Physiology	• How did you feel inside?
Emotions	• How did you feel emotionally?
Behaviour	• What did you do? What happened?
Heart	• What did you *really* want out of the situation?
Biblical wisdom	• Where is God in this situation? How would it look to do things God's way rather than your way? What promise from his word speaks into this situation?
Action	• What would it look like for you to turn back to God in repentance, and then to step out in faith, trusting him as you live his way? What is stopping you?

6
The fears

Do not let your hearts be troubled and do not be afraid.
John 14:27

The fears are emotions rooted in future-oriented thinking that incorporate themes of threat and vulnerability. The cluster includes feelings of dread, panic, distress, nervousness, unease, helplessness, anxiety, feeling overwhelmed, worry and insecurity. Severe forms of anxiety can manifest as phobias, generalised anxiety disorder, panic attacks, eating disorders, obsessive compulsive disorders and self-harm.

Nationally, including within the church, I believe fear in the form of anxiety is something that is increasing at an astonishing rate and I suspect is only going to continue to rise. Anxiety is what I would like to focus on here.

Thoughts

How we think when we are anxious is shown by the associated destructive thought patterns. They are those thoughts that take on the form of 'what if?' thinking, followed by the assumption of an inevitable catastrophe. Mentally it is the acronym **F**alse **E**vidence **A**ppearing **R**eal in action! Anxiety typically manifests in three main areas: fear of man, fear over lack of provision and fear because of health concerns. Cognitive distortions often present include:

- **All-or-nothing thinking:** We have rigid and extreme attitudes, such as, 'If I don't pass the test, I'll never cope'
- **Magnification:** We look for evidence that overestimates the degree of threat
- **Emotional reasoning:** We feel a certain way, and therefore we believe that to be the reality of the situation
- **Mind reading and fortune telling:** We believe we know what people are thinking about us and that it will always be negative. We assume we know what will happen in a situation and that it will always be bad
- **Mental filtering:** We underestimate our ability to cope with the threat

Biology

The physiological changes fears produce are those of the 'flight' mechanism. Physical symptoms may include a very tight stomach with significantly aggravated IBS or digestive problems. Sleep patterns are disturbed, leading to us feeling physically exhausted. Other common symptoms are: a suppressed appetite; breathlessness; palpitations; trembling; sweating, cold and clammy hands; over-breathing; and dizziness. If we are struggling with fear, we will also feel an overwhelming urge to flee.

Behaviour

The behavioural tendencies of anxiety are those of withdrawal. We may avoid people or situations. Our lifestyle may become increasingly restrictive or repetitive as we constantly seek control and reassurance. As we tighten our control, depression often develops. We might try to numb the emotions through drugs or alcohol or by self-harming. We will feel unable to concentrate and may dread things. We will be utterly consumed by the matter that is concerning us, ruminating on it over and over again.

Good or bad fears?

Like the angry emotions, not everything identified in the spectrum of fear is a problem. It is right to show healthy concern over an uncertain health diagnosis or the fact that our new business may not survive initial cash-flow troubles. Biblically, we are right to be alert and to listen to fears, provided we question them through the lens of Scripture. Proverbs 3:21 says, 'My son, do not let wisdom and understanding out of your sight, preserve sound judgment and discretion'. Fear equips us to take action where we can. It can alert us to the need to have wisdom and discernment about situations affecting us. Thus there are times when we are right to listen to fears. However, these emotions become an issue when they take over and start leading us to see everything through a fear filter, even when self-protection isn't necessary.

Sadly, much fear we experience is bad and our anxiety escalates way beyond a healthy concern. We are looking for certainty when there is none. Our anxiety reveals our vulnerabilities and has a tendency towards both underestimating our ability to cope and overestimating the likely danger. As we worry, the thoughts repeatedly go round and round in our heads, yet rather than helping us to deal with the issue, our ruminations reduce our ability to do anything constructive. This can progress to the daily debilitation of generalised anxiety disorder (GAD) and full-blown, frequent panic attacks. In these there is a belief that something terrible or catastrophic will happen *right now*, bringing about acute dread and terror. Often the feared event takes the form of a powerful, threatening mental image, for example imagining a bomb explosion on a tube train when stopped in a tunnel for signals.

The heart

Many people suffer from anxiety for a long time because they are so fearful of seeking help. They also often stall in therapy because they are so scared about stepping out of their comfort zone. The need to control prevents them from taking the necessary steps to increase their low frustration tolerance to emotional discomfort. They must instead learn to trust God and let go of their desire to be in control. This is why getting to the heart matter is so vital. It reveals what we are thinking about ourselves, others and about God and hence what we are truly worshipping.

What is dominating the heart when we are anxious? What is the heart matter? When we look through the lens of Scripture, this reveals a heart that *fails to trust in God* and therefore must be in *control*. Maybe we fear losing our job or possessions or our money? Are we frightened of losing our health? Are we frightened of other people and what they think of or say to us? Are we concerned whether they will reject us? The bottom line is that when our heart refuses to fully trust our heavenly Father, we desperately look to ourselves or put our trust in other people or things instead. But people will inevitably fail us and expose our vulnerability, and then the danger is that we will see the need to exert even more control. We trust in other things more than we trust in God, the Creator and Sustainer of all things.

When I Am Afraid is a fantastic anxiety workbook by Ed Welch,[1] which I'd highly recommend. In it Welch states that God's grace is God's manna of the New Testament. In the Old Testament God faithfully provided manna for the Israelites on their long journey through the wilderness. He provided exactly what they needed, at precisely the time they needed it. Likewise, God provides us with exactly what we need – his grace – and when he knows we need it. However, if we view tomorrow's troubles without being sure of God's grace, of course we will be anxious.

Corrie ten Boom, in her book *The Hiding Place*,[2] speaks of a time when, as a young girl, she was very anxious and fearful about death but her very wise father told her this story:

'Corrie ... when you and I go to Amsterdam – when do I give you your [train] ticket?'
I sniffed a few times, considering this.
'Why, just before we get on the train.'
'Exactly. And our wise Father in heaven knows when we're going to need things too. Don't run out ahead of Him, Corrie. When the time comes that some of us will have to die, you will look into your heart and find the strength you need – just in time.'

This wonderfully depicts what God does. He will give us the grace we need to cope with a difficult situation, *exactly* when we need it and not a moment too soon. Instead of looking inwards to ourselves to control our lives, or outwards to others for help, we must look upwards to the grace of Jesus. If we don't, instead of walking forward as Christians on the narrow path, our difficult emotions will lead us to get trapped in a spiral, whereby we go round and round in circles and sometimes even go backwards.

'Know that I am God'

We feel most anxiety when we feel out of control in a situation. But ultimately we don't have total control over what happens; only God does. He equips us and others with abilities and resources to help us do what we are able to in difficult situations. He gives us direct access in prayer to himself, the Creator of the world. He is the one who sustains the next breath we take. He is in complete and perfect control and he loves us. He only desires what is best for us, as Romans 8:28 reassures us: 'we know that in all things God works for the good of those who love him, who have been called according to his purpose.' We can reduce our anxiety by letting go of something that is bothering us and taking it to God, as Philippians 4:6 tells us: 'Do not be anxious about anything, but in every situation, by prayer and petition, with thanksgiving, present your requests to God.' Of course, the key is then to leave our troubles there with him, rather than bringing them straight back with us.

We live in a society where we are hungry for knowledge and it is more readily available to us than ever before. But with that comes a desire to believe we can control everything through having more knowledge. We can't. There are things we will never understand because we are not God. Yet we can live from our hearts the words of David: 'When I am afraid, I put my trust in you' (Psalm 56:3).

Therefore, we must examine our hearts of control before the throne of grace and bring these destructive emotions of fear to the foot of the cross. There God gently whispers to us, 'Do not fear; I will help you' (Isaiah 41:13). As we face fear, we must turn away from ourselves and towards the living God, knowing who we are in him because of what he has done at the cross for us. This equips and motivates us to step out in faith, trusting in his promises and letting go of our fears. We can live in the light of the truth of Psalm 46:10 where God says, 'Be still, and know that I am God'. What wonderfully reassuring words they are!

Case study

Julie was thirty-nine years old and married, with three teenage children. Both she and her husband were faithful believers and active in many areas of their church. She worked part-time in professional services as well as caring for her immediate and wider family who lived locally.

She came to see me with anxiety, which primarily manifested itself in the workplace and specifically towards those in management. However, in others areas of her life this anxiety was also noted with people she perceived as having authority over her. She appeared to monitor the possibility of threat excessively. She suffered identity and self-esteem issues, which resulted in feelings of shame and fears she might be publicly revealed as incompetent. Spiritually she complained of feeling a 'separateness' from God.

Thoughts / primary cognitive styles

- Minimisation
- Overly demanding thinking
- Mental filtering
- Mind reading and fortune telling

Biology / physiology

- Agitated and unable to calmly relax
- Poor sleep
- Tight stomach
- Blotches on neck and blushing

Behaviour

- Whilst most people would consider her to be highly competent, she often sought reassurance from others about what she was doing or decisions she needed to make for fear of disapproval
- She adopted avoidance strategies around managers she felt vulnerable with
- She ruminated over current issues or those that had happened in the past, thinking over what she should have done differently

- She was putting a huge amount of pressure on herself to perform to higher standards in order to avoid potential criticism, mistakes and failures

The heart of the matter

During various sessions, the theme of her exerting control in order to prevent shame came out more and more. Even discussing matters caused an elevated 'flight' response. In one session we had a breakthrough moment when she realised that God knew all her mistakes and still loved her – she didn't have to be perfect for him. He was in complete control of the mistakes too and could bring good out of them. She sat looking stunned as she suddenly understood this. She had been working so hard to control things so as to avoid making mistakes that would 'let God down in some way'.

However, the theme of shame kept emerging and eventually a few events involving a person in authority over her came to the surface. She felt she had dealt with these issues a long time ago, so it was frustrating to her that they were coming out again now. But as we spoke about how she'd dealt with them, it became apparent that she had essentially 'buried the thoughts into a box', albeit in the guise of 'the arms of Jesus'. If she didn't ever think about them, she felt OK; if she did think about them, emotionally she struggled greatly.

The heart of the matter was her desire to *control* keeping this matter separate from her. This resulted in her feeling separate from God. She had suppressed those parts from her past she didn't like, instead of accepting God had given those difficult situations to her for a reason, and he loved her entirely – including where her behaviour had been unpleasant. She only felt acceptable to God if she presented the 'good' bits. 'How do I know I can trust God with the bad bits?' she asked at a crucial point.

> I answered, 'Do you not think that someone who gave up his beloved Son to die for you and set you free is someone who can be entirely trusted with the "whole" you, including the bad bits?'

How about you?

Consider the questions below regarding a situation about which you are feeling anxious.

Situation	• What / who made you anxious?
Thoughts	• What did you think?
Physiology	• How did you feel inside?
Emotions	• How did you feel emotionally?
Behaviour	• What did you do? What happened?
Heart	• What did you *really* want out of the situation?
Biblical wisdom	• Where is God in this situation? How would it look to do things God's way rather than your way? What promise from his word speaks into this situation?
Action	• What would it look like for you to turn back to God in repentance, and then to step out in faith, trusting him as you live his way? What is stopping you?

7

The tears

> ***May the God of hope fill you with all joy and peace as you trust in him, so that you may overflow with hope by the power of the Holy Spirit.***
>
> *Romans 15:13*

Our third emotional cluster is the 'tears': those emotions rooted in loss. The group includes disappointment, hurt, despair, guilt, alienation, isolation, hopelessness, unhappiness, lack of joy, rejection and misery, plus the most severe manifestation of this cluster which is, of course, depression.

There are many excellent Christian books available on depression and I couldn't possibly do justice to such a difficult and complex topic in this small section. So instead I would like to look here at how the tbH model applies to the lack of joy in the Christian life that sadly seems to affect many people in the church today, including many church leaders.

Thoughts

How we think when gripped by joylessness is revealed by the associated destructive thought patterns. They are thoughts that take on the form of 'What's the point?' thinking, which is bleak, burdened and indecisive. Cognitive distortions often present include:

- **Mental filtering:** We see only negative aspects of loss or failure
- **Emotional reasoning:** We feel no joy and therefore believe the situation is joyless
- **Minimisation:** We believe the future is wearing and burdensome or deny that we have done any good – 'All that work, for nothing; hardly anyone came'
- **Over-generalisation:** We attribute one discouragement to many situations, such as along the lines of, 'What's the point? No-one else ever bothers; it's always down to me'
- **Mind reading and fortune telling:** We make negative predictions about what people think about us and the hopelessness of the future

Biology

If we are experiencing the 'tears', we can react in different ways. We may feel a low-level 'flight' response as we want to escape, or we might feel a low-level 'fight' response as we feel angry at others or at the situation for burdening us. We may just feel nothing at all and begrudgingly go through the motions. Other manifestations might include a tight stomach, IBS symptoms, being aggravated, an affected appetite or disturbed sleep patterns. In one sense there may be a 'physical nothingness' about the joylessness; but in another sense it can involve a mixture of lots of uncomfortable physical sensations.

Behaviour

The behavioural tendencies of joylessness often include withdrawal. Such people are sometimes negative about situations or people, frequently fearing the possibility of extra burdens, so try to avoid them. Sometimes they display signs of frustration and bitterness in outward grumbling at or about others. Sometimes they experience extreme sadness and weepiness. When someone is joyless, they can lose their pleasure and interest in things that had previously been pleasurable to them. Everything feels pointless. They might therefore withdraw from these things and go more deeply into themselves. They may also begin to display an attitude of going through the motions but out of a sense of duty, drudgery or feeling burdened about serving the Lord. As a result the joyless person might become resentful and unable to worship because God can seem a million miles away from the daily drudgery. Procrastination is also a common behaviour. This is because low frustration tolerance (LFT) is pronounced for such people and reflects their perceived belief that they are no longer able to tolerate unpleasant feelings such as frustration, boredom or setbacks. They feel sad and overwhelmed but also unmotivated, believing the tasks ahead simply cannot be contemplated.

Good or bad tears?

Like the other clusters of emotions, not everything identified in the spectrum of tears is a problem. For example, the extreme sadness of grief in bereavement is a normal response created by a significant loss. In a sense, we can also experience a very real and understandable 'grief' response when we are involved in a church split or there are severe relational difficulties between believers. We should mourn when this happens, as God does when he sees it. In a different way, if we are joyless, this could be due to too many demands on our time and could usefully alert us to the need to delegate some of our workload, requesting help and support from leadership and our wider church family. This is a sign of wisdom and strength, not weakness. These are all healthy but joyless responses to experience and it is right that we should feel them, listen to them and take appropriate action. When we do take those steps gradually, joy in the Christian walk does return, sometimes very dramatically.

In contrast, however, feeling no joy in the absence of any trial, or the unhappy joylessness that is felt by Christians who feel chronically overburdened, is never right. In these cases serving has become full of duty and drudgery, and our relationships and ministry are suffering because of it. We become tetchy and defensive, and we're overly sensitive to comments. We feel grumpy and then guilty. Distorted thought patterns occur. Indeed, joylessness and spiritual burnout can involve the same negative triad of thinking that appears in depression: the negative view of yourself, the world and the future. But it also involves our wrong thinking about God.

The heart

God uses trials, including suffering the trial of joylessness, to transform our hearts and renew our minds into the likeness of his Son. This is God's ultimate plan for us. If we expect God to be our 'fairy Godfather' and wave a heavenly wand to give us back our joy, we have created an identity for him to suit our purposes. We've made him just a bit more powerful than us, having the same thoughts and ways that we have. But God is not like us; he doesn't think or behave like us. He loves us more than we can ever imagine and he works in ways of which we could never even dream. He wants us to look, see and understand his awesome glory, and worship him fully. Ed Welch summarises this so well when he states, 'If Jesus doesn't surprise you, then you haven't met him yet.'[1] The truth that God wants our whole hearts, not our half hearts, is made strikingly clear in the angel's words to the church in Ephesus in Revelation 2:2–4:

I know your deeds, your hard work and your perseverance. I know that you cannot tolerate wicked people, that you have tested those who claim to be apostles but are not, and have found them false. You have persevered and have endured hardships for my name, and have not grown weary. Yet I hold this against you: you have forsaken the love you had at first.

If we are experiencing an outer burdened joylessness, this reveals that we have lost our first love too. But God is calling us back to him. He wants our whole hearts so much that in love he may ask us to walk the hard path of joyless burden to show us that he can provide us with so much more than this world has to offer. This is our certain hope; this world is not all there is. One day we will face our Master and hear these words: 'Well done, good and faithful servant!' (Matthew 25:21). Then the new heaven and earth will be ushered in, when, '"There will be no more death" or mourning or crying or pain, for the old order of things has passed away' (Revelation 21:4). We have this sure certain hope, however unfruitful we believe our contribution to kingdom work may have been.

What is dominating the heart when we are joyless? What is the heart matter? It can be more complicated to pinpoint the heart matter in this cluster. However, when we look through the lens of Scripture, this reveals that the root of joylessness is loss. This can be a response to wanting good things, such as for people to come along to church events and to come to a saving faith, but to the wrong degree. Therefore, when these desires fail to happen, we feel their loss deeply and everything can become meaningless. That loss reflects putting our (good) wants ahead of God's perfect timing and plans. Our wants have in fact become our first love and are placed above God.

Choice in loss

It's true to say that there are other factors that contribute to how we think, feel and behave each day: our childhood and upbringing; our health and hormones; our culture; our personality; and our life experiences, especially trauma. But, as gently as I can, I want to show that we *do* have a choice in our loss. Joy is a fruit of the Spirit that we have been given, so even if we feel unhappy – due to very real trials we endure – we still have a choice to experience deep in our heart the joy of knowing forgiveness and living out the new identity we have through a direct relationship with God.

The psalms perfectly illustrate many occasions where there is very real loss but nevertheless there is still a heart-cultivated joy in the power and glory of the Lord. Graham Beynon, in his book *Heart Attitudes*,[2] demonstrates this same cultivated heart attitude of joy with the example of the hymn writer Horatio Spafford. After losing his four daughters at sea, he wrote the lines, 'When peace, like a river, attendeth my way; when sorrows like sea billows roll; whatever my lot, Thou has taught me to say, it is well, it is well with my soul.'[3]

Sometimes the distress of emotional loss and unhappiness stops us from having outward joy. But at these times we need to reflect again on the knowledge that God hasn't left us – even if we feel he has – and know his love for us in our unhappiness and loss. This then allows us to start to see that he is calling to us through our darkness and the loss we feel in our heart.

Case study

Joyce was fifty-five years old and had been a widow for some years. She served diligently at the church and was active in everything. She was generally considered friendly and easy to get along with and felt she had many friends.

She came to see me feeling unhappy, joyless and burdened but not depressed. Recently, everything was seeming pointless and a chore to her. She lacked energy and zeal. Most worryingly for her, relationships that had once been very good were now feeling very tense. She also felt God was so far away and spiritually her life wasn't good. She couldn't seem to read her Bible anymore, or if she did, it meant nothing to her. Her worship was cold and empty, as she simply 'went through the motions'. Nor did she feel able to pray any longer.

Thoughts / primary cognitive styles

- Emotional reasoning
- Mental filtering
- Overly demanding thinking
- All-or-nothing thinking

Biology / physiology

- Notably agitated
- Disturbed sleep patterns
- Lack of appetite
- Speech fast and in an elevated pitch
- Frequent red blotches coming up her neck when talking about difficult events

Behaviour

- She dreaded going out to meetings for fear of what people might ask her to do, so was avoiding them
- She also avoided friends because they kept asking if she was OK and this made her feel angry. She knew she had spoken very critically to a few of them recently
- She lacked energy and zeal and didn't want to be part of any of the usual activities, which now seemed so futile

The heart of the matter

Driving everything was a heart that worshipped her desire for good things, such as the church always looking nice and therefore people bringing flowers and helping with the cleaning, as well as of course people coming along to events. But her (good) wants had become heart needs; they had become more important to her than her desire for her personal relationship with God and her brothers and sisters in Christ. These relationships were therefore suffering greatly. Although she served and served, other people didn't see church in quite the same way as she did so she became bitter and critical of them. Serving had become a burden and a chore, and was also causing her to sink spiritually as she mourned the loss of those heart needs which weren't happening. In the process she had lost the ability to worship her first love, Jesus Christ. She was unable to pray, rarely read the Bible anymore and struggled to even sing hymns in church.

How about you?

Consider the questions below regarding a situation about which you are feeling joyless and burdened.

Situation
- What are you feeling joyless about?

Thoughts
- What did you think?

Physiology
- How did you feel inside?

Emotions
- How did you feel emotionally?

Behaviour
- What did you do? What happened?

Heart
- What did you *really* want out of the situation?

Biblical wisdom
- Where is God in this situation? How would it look to do things God's way rather than your way? What promise from his word speaks into this situation?

Action
- What would it look like for you to turn back to God in repentance, and then to step out in faith, trusting him as you live his way? What is stopping you?

8

The battleground of our heart

Whoever wants to be my disciple must deny themselves and take up their cross daily and follow me.

Luke 9:23

The Christian walk on the narrow path is sometimes a very hard one, especially when we are in the grip of difficult emotional states such as bitterness, anxiety or joylessness. Why? It is because there is a spiritual battle raging on and the battleground is our hearts. The reality is that we are constantly being tempted to trust in things other than God, even if we're not actively aware of it. Our hearts are deceptive above all things. They are constantly luring us into thinking the usually good *wants* of our hearts are actually *needs* we can't do without.

Wants or needs?

In day-to-day language we may use these two terms interchangeably, but spiritually there is a big difference between them. There is nothing wrong with wanting to be loved or accepted or healthy, or to know we can provide for our families, or even to be able to plan for righteous hoped-for futures. The problem starts when those wants become elevated to perceived needs or what the Bible would term desires.

When we want something and it happens, we are delighted and thankful. However, if a 'want' – as opposed to a 'need' – doesn't happen, though we can feel disappointed, we quickly accept that it was not God's plan for us and move on.

The same is not true of those things we believe to be our needs. When something becomes a need, our lives become ruled by it. It affects the functional beliefs and loyalties of our heart. The need leads us naively along and determines the will of our heart. It hijacks our hearts and motivates us throughout our days, dictating our thoughts, emotions and behaviours. When something has become elevated to a need, you might hear expressions like, 'I couldn't stand it I don't get this promotion,' or 'If I didn't have her, I couldn't bear it.'

If our need is met, emotionally that makes us feel great. The need has become a part of our created identity and we find ourselves being affirmed on the basis of having our need fulfilled. However, if the need isn't met, is threatened or we have it but then lose it, we can hit an emotional rock bottom. Since we have placed our need before God in terms of importance, it captures our heart loyalties and subtly lures us away from following him. We worship our need instead of finding our satisfaction and purpose in God and desiring what he wants for us.

How Satan exploits our desires

In all this spiritual fallout from unfulfilled needs, Satan is very much at work. He is active in turning good things, such as us wanting to be loved or to have a peaceful life, into personal needs. He then uses these needs to entice us away from loving God and delighting in living his way, whatever that may be for us.

For example, Satan rarely tries in just one step to persuade a married person to commit adultery. He knows that most people's immediate reaction to this suggestion would be to say 'no' and flee from the possibility. He's far too clever for such an obvious tactic. Instead, he taps into the often good wants of someone's heart, such as their desire to be loved and valued. Then, little by little, he persuades them just to make eye contact across a crowded gym, just to have coffee together, just to swap mobile numbers, just to send a message, just to go for a walk together, just to delete that flirtatious email chain so their spouse won't see, and so on. As those tiny steps are achieved, suddenly the step into physical intimacy isn't that far away anymore. Furthermore, the *want* of being loved has turned into a *need* for emotional and physical affirmation from this person to whom they are not married. Then this need begins to subtly rule them and overrule God.

A reminiscent problem?

In the opening chapter of Genesis, we read God spoke his will and it came to be, and it was good. Out of love and a desire for us to enjoy all that he has to give, he created Adam and then Eve as his helper, and it was 'very good' (1:31). In the creational account of Genesis 1 the refrain 'God' (or *Elohim* in the original Hebrew) is used, meaning the all-powerful, mighty and strong Creator. However, as soon as his relationship with humans comes to be described, from Genesis 2:4, 'LORD God' or 'Yahweh' is the name given. This is his covenantal personal name, which is consistently expressed to reflect his presence, accessibility and intimacy with Adam and Eve.

This is important to understand when, in Genesis 3, Satan tempts Eve by asking her, 'Did God really say, "You must not eat from any tree in the garden"?' (v. 1). Can you see the subtlety of what has happened here? Not only has Satan twisted God's words, putting destructive thoughts into Eve's mind, but he has manipulated them in another clever way too – 'LORD God' and its implications of personal intimacy within a covenant relationship has gone, to be replaced by 'God'. Look at the impact this has on Eve in verses 2-3: 'The woman said to the snake, "We may eat fruit from the trees in the garden, but God did say, 'You must not eat fruit from the tree that is in the middle of the garden, and you must not touch it, or you will die.'"' Eve knows what she shouldn't do but Satan has subtly broken down the knowledge of her intimate relationship with the 'Lord God'; when that is removed, her God-given identity is distorted and it is far easier to disobey. Satan has exploited Eve's good want of having knowledge of good and evil, which the 'Lord God' ordained to be learned in personal relationship with him. Instead he has turned this into a need lived out through a fallen relationship with God and a distorted identity.

Satan doesn't tell her to be disobedient but subtly tempts her through her heart's desires and erodes her relationship with the 'Lord God'. Thus, Eve's functional beliefs in her heart are changed. Eve and then Adam worship their 'need' to be like God, having knowledge of good and evil, more than they worship the living God himself. The will of their hearts becomes focused on achieving that need through their thoughts, biology, emotions and behaviour.

That initial temptation, which led to the Fall and all its consequences, is remarkably similar to how Satan exploits our desires today. He erodes our intimacy with the 'Lord God' and the security of our identity we have in him, and turns the good wants in our hearts into the idols of heart needs.

Our way or God's way?

The ultimate question for us all, including when we are in the grip of overwhelming emotions, is: Who are we going to worship? Ourselves or God? Are we going to live our way or God's way? Which will we choose? The desires we worship in our heart determine our choice. That is why part of any pastoral care for those struggling with difficult emotions must be to uncover what that person truly wants out of the situation. This reveals their heart's desires and immediately brings the situation onto a more biblical footing, which allows us to see how the person is oscillating between living their way or God's way.

James, brother of Jesus, writes to believers, 'Submit yourselves, then, to God. Resist the devil, and he will flee from you. Come near to God and he will come near to you. Wash your hands, you sinners, and purify your hearts, you double-minded' (James 4:7–8). This expression 'double-minded' refers to someone living with one foot in the world and the other in God. And this is what we do when we are in the grip of difficult emotions. We trust Jesus as our Saviour but we don't see him as Lord over our lives. We need to remember that Jesus is indeed Lord of our lives. Then we need to examine how the knowledge of that should reorient our hearts and hence renew our minds, our emotions and our behaviours. Christ is living and active in every moment we face in life. Whether we realise it or not, we are constantly making a decision to face this moment either our way or his way. If we choose our way, this means acting on the flesh and allowing our sinful natures to worship, run after and trust in things other than God. We have, in other words, answered, 'You're not Lord of my life; I am.' Yet if we live God's way, this means grabbing hold of what he *has* done for us, what he *will* do for us, and also what he *is* doing for us right now. Knowing who he is and who we have become – because of what he has done – means taking him at his word and grasping tightly onto his promises. We turn to him, pray to him and follow him obediently in faith, *even* if emotionally this feels hard to do.

We are told that Christians must 'take up their cross daily' as they follow Christ (Luke 9:23). The trial of living with difficult emotions can certainly feel a huge burden to carry. But it is so easy to believe that we are at the mercy of our emotions, being utterly led by them, and as a result life can quickly look very bleak. What we often forget, especially during the times we most need to remember, is that through the Holy Spirit dwelling within us, we are never alone. If we have trusted in the life, death and resurrection of Jesus Christ, he is lifting up the bit of the cross that is dragging along the ground because we're not strong enough to lift it ourselves. He has that strength when we don't. As the apostle Paul writes, 'But he [God] said to me, "My grace is sufficient for you, for my power is made perfect in weakness." Therefore I will boast all the more gladly about my weaknesses, so that Christ's power may rest on me' (2 Corinthians 12:9). Moreover, as Christ shines his strength and grace into our brokenness and suffering, we are transformed more and more into his glorious likeness.

We are not in this battle alone. Provided we turn away from the power of our emotion and instead look to Christ, trusting in the promises of his word, his Spirit in us can free us from the grip of powerful emotions. Consequently:

- If we are gripped by *sneers*, we can be released from the pride in our heart and freed from our anger and bitterness through knowing *humility* from God
- If we are gripped by *fears*, we can be released from the need to control in our heart and freed from our fear through truly *trusting God*
- If we are gripped by *tears*, we can be released from the loss in our heart and freed from our joylessness by knowing the certain *hope* we have in Christ for the future, both in this life and in the next

Whole hearts or half hearts?

How will we respond to this choice of how to live? How will we decide to worship God? Will we worship him wholeheartedly?

Or will we worship him only partially? Would we like to be free from particular perceived needs or desires? Or, if we're honest, do we really like the comfort our desires bring, wanting only to be rid of the dislike of their unpleasant consequences? Have we, in the words of Paul, 'exchanged the truth about God for a lie, and worshipped and served created things rather than the Creator – who is for ever praised. Amen' (Romans 1:25)?

When we worship our perceived need more than we worship God, though we profess Jesus as our Lord and Saviour, in truth we trust him for our salvation but not as Lord over everything in our lives. We believe he is the perfect judge, but we don't trust him to deal with someone who has greatly angered or hurt us. We know he is in control of everything, but we cannot sleep due to worry over a relationship. We believe we will have an eternity with him in heaven, but we doubt he is with us now in our feelings of loss. Though we believe his promises with our heads, the desire of our personal needs prevents us from connecting this to our hearts. This then causes us to live out our needs through our emotions, thoughts and behaviours.

God isn't satisfied with such half-hearted worship. He doesn't want our outer facade of 'religion'; he calls for our whole hearts. He doesn't just want to make us less broken and put a plaster over our suffering; he wants the real inner us to be transformed into the likeness of his Son. We must remember that when we put our trust in Jesus' death on the cross as our Saviour, we surrendered to Jesus being the Lord over our entire lives too. God is not a bigger and better version of us, wanting what we want; God's biggest desire and purpose for us is to make us more like Jesus. He wants this more than he wants us to be happy or released from taxing emotions such as anxiety or anger. Indeed, he often uses the trials of emotional suffering to show us those needs plaguing our hearts.

At all times, but especially when the darkness of our difficult emotions engulfs us, we should keep looking upwards to God. We read in Numbers 21 the account of the Israelites as they wandered in the desert having been freed from slavery in Egypt. Although God had rescued Israel and promised them the land of Canaan, they grew impatient and began complaining against God and Moses. In his displeasure, God's response was to send venomous snakes amongst them. Many were bitten and died. Then the people confessed their grumbling to Moses and begged him to pray for mercy. As Numbers 21:8 tells us, 'The LORD said to Moses, "Make a snake and put it up on a pole; anyone who is bitten can look at it and live."' That's all they had to do. Rather than looking inwards, remembering the provision they had 'enjoyed' as slaves, they had to look outwards and upwards to the snake on the pole. If they obeyed God's command, they would live.

We can be like that in suffering too. So often we look inwards to ourselves. As we become introspective, we close our eyes to God. We say he has left us because we can't feel him, when the truth is that he's so close to us in our suffering, speaking into our hearts in a sometimes tiny whisper. 'For God, who said, "Let light shine out of darkness," made his light shine in our hearts to give us the light of the knowledge of God's glory displayed in the face of Christ' (2 Corinthians 4:6).

9

Looking outwards, looking upwards

Trust in the* Lord *with all your heart and lean not on your own understanding; in all your ways submit to him, and he will make your paths straight.

Proverbs 3:5–6

Looking upwards to God

When we are in the grip of broken emotions and our minds are full of emotional turmoil, it can feel very hard to pray and read the Bible. Our exhaustion and disturbed sleep patterns stop us coming to church regularly. Our doubts and self-recrimination stop us taking communion in good conscience. We avoid people so we don't have to answer their question, 'How are you?'

Yet Bible reading, prayer, church fellowship and communion are some of the means of grace that God has given us to help us remain close to him. When we engage in them, we are more in tune with the Spirit as he controls our hearts. Conversely, as soon as we let go of these means of grace, it is instead our sinful nature that has a grip on the steering wheel of our lives.

Who's driving?

I once heard a sermon where the preacher painted a really helpful picture that has stuck with me. Imagine you're driving a car and your sinful nature is at the steering wheel. When people get in the way, you blast on the horn and yell unpleasantly out the window at people to get them out of your way. Then, one day, you come to know Christ as your own personal Lord and Saviour. He gives you the gift of his Holy Spirit to permanently reside in your heart. Now it is the Spirit who sits in the driver's seat and takes hold of the steering wheel, driving your life.

However, your sinful nature is still there. Admittedly, it's been pushed across into the passenger seat, but it's still trying to grab at the steering wheel to pull you off track. How much you depend on the means of God's grace to you determines whether your sinful nature will be successful at pulling the wheel away from the Spirit. If you are not regularly coming under God's word, praying to him, trusting him, knowing who you are in him and enjoying fellowship with him, your sinful nature will take control. Then, once your sinful nature has the wheel, you are left more susceptible to sin through not only overt disobedience but also subtler ways you may not even be fully aware of because of the deceit of your hearts.

Our loving heavenly Father knows when we are struggling and suffering. By looking upwards to him, we can enjoy the means of his grace to remain close to him. We can use the armour of God he provides for protection against inevitable spiritual attack (see Ephesians 6:10–17). We can listen to what he is revealing about our hearts and, by submitting to the truths we learn from, be freed from the grip of difficult emotions. This isn't easy but in God's strength it is possible. However, we need to be intentional about taking action to bring about emotional change.

Looking outwards for others

We can also help others in their emotional turbulence, as well as expecting to be helped ourselves in this way too. We are all on this walk together – there is no 'them' and 'us' – and this truth works both ways. Ed Welch expresses it so beautifully in his book *Side by Side* where he writes that since life is hard, we – all of us – are needy and we are needed.[1]

There are many ways in which we can support others in their need, but below are some biblical principles that are key and have been gleaned primarily from a whole range of material produced by CCEF (the Christian Counseling & Education Foundation) and Biblical Counselling UK. More specifically, I would highly recommend Paul Tripp's book *Instruments in the Redeemer's Hands*[2] which provides wisdom and sound biblical guidance about, as his subtitle states, 'people in need of change helping people in need of change'.

Speak the truth in love (Ephesians 4:15)

If someone is stuck in the grip of difficult emotions, we must show them biblical love. True biblical love involves the following (often difficult) conversations:

- Gently speaking the truth in love and helping them to examine their hearts against God's word
- Asking them to consider what God may be saying to them through their emotions
- Encouraging them to consider how their thoughts and behaviour might be acting as an emotional smoke alarm to alert them to issues they need to address
- Prompting them to ask what God is revealing about this part of their heart they have not given over to his loving hand
- Helping them to ponder, 'Does this Lord live right now, in this moment?' Given that the answer is yes, what does that change?
- Directing them to their identity in Christ and the relevance of the gospel to their particular struggle. Our identity is not our struggle or emotional state

Of course, people need our time, willingness to listen, practical support and prayers too. But love without speaking the truth at a heart level is not biblical love. This true love requires great wisdom, prayer, courage, grace and sensitivity, spoken from a heart motivated only by compassion and desiring restoration and transformation. It can be very hard to do. Simply praying for their trial of difficult emotion to be removed isn't enough. We must imitate the work of Christ and love them *enough* to point them to God's words that are directed at their hearts – in order to help them to be conformed to Jesus' likeness through the sanctifying power of the Spirit.

Trust God's word because it will never return empty handed (Isaiah 55:11)

When we truly trust something, we act on it. It doesn't just remain a passive knowledge; it motivates us to action. I have high cholesterol. Blood tests set off a 'health smoke detector', highlighting that I had a problem. When I was called in to discuss it, the doctor explained to me what the long-term consequences of those results were. She gave me some guidelines as to what I could do to improve it. She then sent me off to put into practice what she had told me to do.

I believe the medical tests. I respect my doctor's views and experience. I trust advice from the British Heart Foundation. If I ignored it all, I would be a complete fool. Instead I've listened to all I've been told and put it into practice. I have become focused on the problem and have an awareness of it in my life. My thoughts have changed and my frequency of and desire for tucking into fish and chips with gusto has reduced.

But how do we fare when it comes to trusting God at *his* word? What do we really believe about the Bible? It is, of course, God's inspired word speaking to us. The doctrine of Scripture tells us that it is sufficient for all we face in life and it equips us to live our lives in faithful obedience to him. The Bible provides objective truth about everything we face in our postmodern world, which instead encourages us to live according to the subjective reality of what feels to be true for me. If we truly grasped these biblical truths, our desire would be to connect the Bible more to the trials we experience in life and to long to put its teaching into practice in our lives. Psalm 12:6 describes it like this: '… the words of the LORD are flawless, like silver purified in a crucible, like gold refined seven times.' No-one would try to re-purify silver that was already pure, but for emphasis David describes God's words as being refined seven times, the number of perfection and completeness.

The reality, though, is that as Christians we can have two different types of knowledge: that in our head and that in our heart. We can know we are supposed to love others because, as we have already seen, Jesus answers a question about which are the most important commandments by saying: '"Love the Lord your God with all your heart and with all your soul and with all your mind and with all your strength." "The second is this: "Love your neighbour as yourself." There is no commandment greater than these' (Mark 12:30–31). But do we really 'know' this with our hearts?

We can recall it as knowledge because we have heard it many times and perhaps memorised it. Yet it is only when we live it out through experience that it truly penetrates our hearts and lives. In turn, how we live our lives is the best indicator of what is going on in our hearts and how much we truly know Jesus as our Lord and Saviour. There is a direct connection between our daily thoughts, behaviours and emotions and our relationship with God. What we see outpouring into our horizontal relationships with others reflects our vertical relationship with God.

Show love and compassion in practical ways (James 2:17)

In 1 Kings 19:1–9 we see Elijah fleeing from Jezebel's threats after slaughtering the prophets of Baal. He's afraid and says, 'I have had enough, Lord … Take my life; I am no better than my ancestors' (v. 4). Then he lays down under the bush and falls asleep. God graciously sends an angel to minister to Elijah. Elijah rests and then he eats and drinks what the angel has provided to strengthen him, before continuing his journey – one of forty days and nights to Horeb.

This is a wonderfully compassionate illustration of the fact that we worship a practical God who knows and loves us, and he knows our limits. We too, albeit in our more limited means, must be practical in showing our love to those suffering emotionally. Here are some suggestions as to how we can do that. We can:

- Simply 'be' with them and listen to them, whilst also encouraging them to, 'Be still, and know that I am God' (Psalm 46:10)
- Pray for them and encourage them to pray with us – using short written liturgy might help them remain focused
- Discreetly (though always honouring confidentiality if requested) ask others to pray for them
- Read the Bible to them, especially the psalms, which demonstrate how to delight in God even in difficult times
- Encourage them to be honest – there is no need for shame
- Point them to seeking medical help, if appropriate, and then help them get to and from medical appointments
- Encourage them to seek pastoral care
- Help to keep them looking outwards and upwards, rather than inwards
- Gently challenge their thinking styles
- Encourage them to try new behaviours, even if they don't feel like it

- Help them to examine God's promises and their certain hope in eternity
- Encourage them to take every unhelpful thought captive
- Prompt them to think God's way, which might mean that their trials are for their spiritual good
- Encourage them to know that feeling and reality are not necessarily the same things
- Take them out and let them into our families
- Arrange meal rotas or help with commitments and chores
- Encourage them to pray for and serve others

In all this, we would be wise to remember three important truths, as follows.

God has determined our identity

There are so many conflicting pulls on our identity in our postmodern society. Facebook, Twitter, Snapchat and our culture's view of marriage, gender and sexuality all subtly infiltrate the church and our lives. Additionally, the longer we endure difficulties, the more we come to see ourselves defined by them. Yet this is not who you are. Rather it forms an important part of who God has created us to be, enabling us to come alongside others with similar struggles, for his glory. Knowing our identity in Christ and encouraging those who are struggling to do the same is crucial. But we forget, and we plunge into the spiralling depths of 'the gospel gap'. We live out our false identity rather than our Christ-given identity.

We remain thankful for the astonishing and miraculous *past* work of God's saving grace in our lives as he justified us and clothed us with Christ's righteousness. We have a certain hope in God's *future* glorifying grace when one day we will open our eyes and gaze at the beautiful face of Christ, hearing the words from

Matthew 25:23: 'Well done, good and faithful servant!' But what about *now*?

What should we believe as we suffer and face difficult emotions? Where is God and his all-surpassing power of the gospel at these times? We must see that his *present* sanctifying grace is as significant in those moments as it was on the day we were saved. But, again, we forget this, and instead we struggle through in the weakness and limited resources that stem from our distorted identity. We eclipse the wonders of his grace, and forgo the opportunity to be transformed and moulded by him.

It is vital, though, to know who we are: a new creation with a brand new identity. The almighty God promises us that, through Christ's death on the cross, we are declared to be:

- Forgiven (Ephesians 1:7)
- Loved (John 3:16)
- Chosen (Ephesians 1:4)
- Adopted (Ephesians (1:5)
- Becoming more like Christ (2 Corinthians 3:18)
- Blessed (Ephesians 1:3)
- Redeemed (Ephesians 1:7)
- Sealed with the Holy Spirit (Ephesians 1:13)
- Blameless in God's sight (Ephesians 1:4)

These all remain true, even on the days we don't feel loved or secure or blessed. When we remember, in the abyss of 'the gospel gap', what Jesus has already done for us and therefore who we are in Christ, it gives us the motivation to live the gospel-centred life he desires. We can live fearlessly, in peace, with thankfulness, courageously and contented. Knowing the scriptural truths concerning who we really are in Christ, we are equipped to obey the scriptural commands about how we should live. Secure in our identity and God's promises, we can live them out in faith and equipped by the power of his indwelling Spirit.

The Greek word for 'power' in the gospel is from where the word 'dynamite' is derived. It denotes explosive power – the kind that turns lives upside down. We are weak jars of clay but we carry the treasure of God's gospel inside us. That gospel has explosive power not just to save but also to change how we respond in each all-consuming struggle we face. 2 Corinthians 3:18 assures us: 'we all, who with unveiled faces contemplate the Lord's glory, are being transformed into his image with ever-increasing glory'.

We cannot live for God in our own strength and by our own efforts, but through his all-surpassing strength and resting on his works. When we are certain of our identity in God, we can let him be the perfect judge when we are angry. We can trust that he is more powerful than anything we are anxious about. And we can rest in the truth that it is our loving heavenly Father who gives, and takes away, when all seems hopeless.

God's ways are not the same as ours

We can have our own ideas about what God should do to help someone suffering. I've mentioned before how our limited view of a situation just wants the trial of emotional distress to be removed. We may look upwards at all the messy threads dangling underneath the tapestry of their or our lives. Our inclination is to ask God to use a heavenly pair of scissors to trim off the untidy bits – and quickly! But in Isaiah 55:8 God declares, 'my thoughts are not your thoughts, neither are your ways my ways'. He, looking down from above, sees the beautifully interwoven tapestry, with everything fitting together in its place. Where we see problems, God only sees parts of his grand plan.

One of the ways God works to do this is through our difficult emotions. We may find this hard to accept but, as 2 Corinthians

1:3–4 tells us, 'Praise be to ... the Father of compassion and the God of all comfort, who comforts us in all our troubles'. Do you really believe that? Just reflect on it for a moment. God sent his only Son to die for us when we were his enemies. How much more love and compassion will he pour out on us when we, now his precious children, are struggling? God can and does heal, sometimes in sudden and astonishing ways. But more often we see him slowly and gently showering us with his love and grace through our struggles. He patiently performs the role of the potter, moulding and shaping us to become more like Jesus. Jeremiah gives us a picture of this where he says, 'So I went down to the potter's house, and I saw him working at the wheel. But the pot he was shaping from the clay was marred in his hands; so the potter formed it into another pot, shaping it as seemed best to him' (Jeremiah 18:3–4).

God is active in our emotions

As we saw at the start of the book, one of our biggest problems is that we focus on the intensity of our emotions and are led by them. Yet there is another way of seeing things. We should instead look upwards and see how God is speaking to us through those emotions. How are they highlighting the parts of our hearts that we have kept from him? Do we have perceived needs to which we are desperately clinging and worshipping? Have they been elevated higher than God, the only one worthy of our worship?

God provides the antidote for our fallen hearts in Scripture, and through his Spirit he gives us the means for conforming to Jesus' likeness in these emotional struggles. This work will never be complete in this life. Only in our eternity with him will we be totally free from the emotional bondage of this world. But we can be changed to be more like him and live for him in the light of the truth of his glorious gospel. What an astonishing witness to others this is when it happens.

Below is a summary of our difficult emotions and heart attitudes, plus where they lead us, and the scriptural truth on which we should reflect in the context of our new and permanent identity we have in Christ.

Emotional Cluster	Heart matter	Typical thoughts	Typical behaviour	For reflection
The sneers	*Pride*	*'I know better'* *'They are wrong; I am right'*	*Complaining* *Bitterness* *Judging others*	*Scripture about humility*
The fears	*Control*	*'But what if …'* *'If that should ever happen, I couldn't cope'*	*Consumed with worry* *Sleep problems* *Restlessness* *Agitation*	*Scripture about trust*
The tears	*Loss*	*'What's the point?'* *'I'm useless'* *'It's always like this'*	*Burdened* *Frustrated* *Life seems pointless* *Low mood*	*Scripture about hope*

Our hearts and God's transforming grace

The last crucial issue to address is how we should respond to all this. You may find it helpful to turn to Appendix 2 and use the tbH model yourself to work through any difficult emotions with which you are struggling. However, there is no such thing as an independent Christian. Change happens in Christian community. Therefore why not consider meeting with a small group of trusted believers and working through some of these issues together, thus benefiting from the gentle observations and wisdom of others?

Above all else, remember to pray, asking God to reveal the depths of your heart to you, and knowing that as he does so, it doesn't change his love for you. Also ask that he would help you to see more of himself and who you are in him. God tells us in James 4:10, 'Humble yourselves before the Lord, and he will lift you up.' We don't do this by simply creating tick lists of outer behavioural changes we must implement, because in our own strength we will fail. Instead, James tells us that the astonishing way in which we are transformed is as 'he [God] gives us more grace' (James 4:6). As we submit our hearts in obedience to God, we enjoy him lavishing more grace onto us. We can then know for ourselves the glorious freedom and peace of submitting our entire heart to God.

It might be that, as you've been reading through this book, you've realised that there are parts of your heart that you are fighting to keep for yourself. If that is so, I would earnestly encourage you to confess the idolatrous needs of your heart and submit them to God. Let Jesus be both your Saviour and the Lord over your *entire* life. He can be trusted with our hearts because only he knows our true needs. I once read the following, which wonderfully captures the image of repentance. However far we've walked away from God, repentance is only ever one step away. All we have to do is to turn around 180 degrees and take one single step back into the open arms of our loving heavenly Father. No matter how much we may lose our grip on God and seek to do things our way, he remains holding onto us firmly and never lets us go. God is the same yesterday, today and forever (see Heb. 13:8). This will never change, even when everything around us is falling apart.

For those of you who are experiencing deep emotional suffering at the moment, please listen ... not to the emotion itself, but to God, because he is speaking to you through your trials: 'Be still, and know that [he is] God' (Psalm 46:10). He hasn't left you, even if you feel that he has. He is revealing your heart to you, and that can feel a very painful process. But in doing so, he is also showing you how much he loves you and cares for you.

If we look outwards to God through our broken emotions, the mirrors of our heart, he will reveal our true heart's desires. As he shines the beauty of his light and love into our broken and dark places, he exposes the real us. He sees the depths of our hearts, and yet he loves us the same. He will show us where we are keeping back parts of our heart for ourselves, when they belong only to him.

As we reflect on the truths of God's faithfulness and worship him in love and adoration, the inner bondage of our heart melts away. As we gaze again upon the cross of Jesus, we see the beauty of his love shining through our emotional brokenness and we are transformed through his grace to become more like him.

My prayer for you, as you come to the end of this book, is the prayer of the apostle Paul to the faithful but struggling believers in Ephesus: 'I pray that the eyes of your heart may be enlightened in order that you may know the hope to which he has called you, the riches of his glorious inheritance in his holy people' (Ephesians 1:18).

Appendix 1

Emotions questionnaire

From the list below, please tick or circle the eight–ten emotions you find yourself most commonly experiencing. Make an instinctive choice, without thinking about it too much.

When you have done that, add up how many corresponding 'T', 'S' and 'F' scores you have and write the totals at the bottom. This will indicate whether your emotions fall most in the 'sneers', 'tears' or 'fears' categories, as explained in chapter 4.

Alienation	T
Isolation	T
Depression	T
Destructive tendencies	S
Disappointment	T
Anxiety	F
Insecurity	T
Dread	F
Hopelessness	T
Distress	F
Unhappiness	T
Nervousness	F
Rejection	T
Worry	F
Frustration	S

Panic	F
Jealousy	S
Hatred	S
Overwhelmedness	F
Loathing	S
Fury	S
Envy	S
Unease	F
Spite	S
Bitterness	S
Resentment	S
Total 'S'	
Total 'F'	
Total 'T'	

Appendix 2

Using the tbH model yourself

You can use the tbH model to work through emotions with which you are struggling. As you answer the questions below, your prevailing heart motive, which is driving everything, should become clearer. Then look honestly at what the Bible says about this inclination of your heart. What promises of God can you turn to?

What was the situation?			
What did I think? ('t')	*What did I feel?*	*What did I do? ('b')*	*What did I really want? ('H')*
•	•	•	•
•	•	•	•
•	•	•	•
What does biblical wisdom say?	*How can this emotion honour God?*	*What behaviours need to change?*	*How does the Bible speak into this desire?*
•	•	•	•

References

1. Emotions as mirrors of the heart

1 Graham Beynon, *Emotions: Living Life in Colour* (IVP, 2012), p. 40.

2 Graham Beynon, *Emotions*, p. 41.

3 This diagram is adapted with kind permission from Graham Beynon, *Emotions*, p. 41.

2. Emotions as spiritual smoke alarms

1 These concepts and ideas were taken from a course taught by Dr David Powlison, CCEF faculty member and Executive Director, entitled 'Theology and Secular Psychology'. The ideas have been adapted and are used with permission from the Christian Counseling & Educational Foundation (CCEF). To learn more about CCEF and Dr Powlison visit www.ccef.org.

2 Timothy S. Lane and Paul David Tripp, *How People Change* (New Growth Press, second edition 2009).

3 These ideas were taken from a course taught by Winston Smith, CCEF faculty member, entitled 'Marriage Counselling'.

4 Laura Story (Mixon), 'Blessings', copyright © 2011 New Spring/Gleaning Publishing/Imagem/Small Stone Media BV (Adm. Song Solutions www.songsolutions.org). All rights reserved. Used by permission.

3. tbH: It's a heart matter!

1 Paul Mallard, *Staying Fresh* (IVP, 2015), pp. 83–84.

4. Suffering: The sneers, the fears and the tears

1 Paul David Tripp, *Instruments in the Redeemer's Hands* (P&R Publishing, 2002), pp. 143–54.

2 Michael Neenan, *Developing Resilience* (Routledge, 2009), pp. 2–3.

5. The sneers

1 David Powlison, *Seeing with New Eyes* (P&R Publishing, 2008), especially chapter 8.

2 Edward T. Welch, *What Do You Think of Me? Why Do I Care?* (New Growth Press, 2011), p. 19.

3 Tim Chester, *Gospel Centred Marriage* (The Good Book Company, 2011), p. 69.

4 Tim Chester, *You Can Change* (IVP, 2008), p. 74.

6. The fears

1 Ed Welch, *When I Am Afraid* (Evangelical Press, 2010).

2 Corrie ten Boom, *The Hiding Place* (Hodder & Stoughton, first published 1971).

7. The tears

1 Edward T. Welch, *What Do You Think of Me? Why Do I Care?*, p. 32.

2 Graham Beynon, *Heart Attitudes* (IVP, 2014).

3 Horatio Spafford, 'It is well with my soul'.

9. Looking upwards, looking outwards

1 Ed Welch, *Side by Side* (Crossway, 2015).

2 Paul David Tripp, *Instruments in the Redeemer's Hands*.

EMOTIONS
MIRRORS OF THE HEART
Catherine Haddow